Introdu...

The stunning medieval fort ... ng
near the mouth of the Afor ... of
mountains, is a designated \ ... te
13thC castle was built for Edward ... s,
and the walls, over ¾ mile in lengtl ... a
new town occupied by English settlei ...c
bridges built by renowned engineers: ......u s graceful suspension
bridge (1822-26) and the adjacent tubular railway bridge built by Robert
Stephenson which opened in 1849. Conwy was once an important port and
boats still continue the town's mussel fishing tradition. Today the estuary
and marina are home to many small pleasure boats and yachts, and the town
remains a mecca for visitors.

Just to the west of Conwy is historic Sychnant Pass and Conwy Mountain,
the first of a series of dramatic hills towering above the coast and the towns
of Llanfairfechan and Penmaenmawr, some scarred by old granite quarries.
Behind these coastal hills is an upland plateau overlooked by the foothills
of the Carneddau mountains. This diverse open upland landscape, once
occupied by early man and now grazed by wild ponies, contains ancient
standing stones and stone circles. It is crossed by an ancient highway, later a
Roman Road, and the more recent waymarked North Wales Path.

The 30 walks in this book explore the area around Conwy, and the
delightful foothills and upland valleys in the northern fringes of the
Snowdonia National Park, using an extensive network of delightful paths and
upland tracks.

The routes, which range from a simple 2 mile beach walk to a 8½ mile
upland walk to Tal-y-fan mountain, are well within the capability of most
people. Many routes contain shorter walk options. *A key feature is that
individual walks can easily be linked with others to provide longer and
more challenging day walks if required.* They follow public rights of way or
permissive paths, and cross Open Access land, and incorporate sections of the
North Wales Path. Walking boots are recommended, along with appropriate
clothing to protect against the elements. Be properly prepared and equipped
for the higher upland walks, and remember that the condition of the paths can
vary according to season and weather!

Each walk has a detailed map and description which enables the route
to be followed without difficulty, but be aware that changes in detail can
occur at any time. The location of each walk is shown on the back cover and
a summary of the key characteristics of each is provided. This includes an
estimated walking time, but allow more time to enjoy the scenery.

Please observe the country code and respect any ancient site visited.
Enjoy your walking!

WALK 1

CONWY

DESCRIPTION A 2½ mile walk (**A**) exploring Conwy, featuring its medieval town walls, quayside, estuary promenade and attractive woodland of Bodlonded Park. Allow about 2 hours. An alternative 1⅓ mile town walls walk (**B**) is included.
START Conwy Visitor Centre [SH 781774] – located near the railway station.

I Head towards a nearby tower then follow a cobbled path through an archway and continue beneath the town walls to reach an old crane at good viewpoint of the castle. Retrace your steps then climb up the tower and walk along the walls. After descending go along the car park edge to the castle entrance and Tourist Information Centre. Descend to the lower entrance and cross to the pavement opposite beneath the castle. Use the nearby Pelican crossing and go through the archway ahead, then continue over Pont Conwy to enjoy views along the estuary. *Nearby are Telford's suspension bridge and Stephenson's tubular railway bridge.* Retrace your steps then descend to the quayside. Go past Conwy Mussels, toilets, the Liverpool Arms and the Smallest House to pass under the walls. Go up the road then turn RIGHT on the signposted North Wales Path. (For **Walk B** continue up to the main road and resume text at point **3**.) Follow Marine Walk past Bodlonded Wood and along the estuary edge. *It was created by Albert Wood, one of Conwy's great benefactors, who lived at nearby Bodlondeb mansion, built for his family in 1877.* Later the walkway bends inland.

2 Shortly, enter the corner of Bodlonded Wood and follow the path ahead up the woodland edge, then turn LEFT up a stepped path. At a crossroad of paths by a seat, follow a path LEFT up to paths by post 14N. Turn LEFT and follow the wide path round the wooded slope, past post 16Q then a seat at a good viewpoint, after which it bends south past a path on the left and rises. Soon take its left fork down the wood edge past post

18C to cross a road behind Bodlonded Hall. Follow formal paths round the left side of the building, then the left edge of parkland to join the road. Follow it to the main road.

3 Turn LEFT through the nearby archway, then go up steps onto the town walls. First descend to the end overlooking the river, then return to follow the western walls up to a corner tower, from where there is a dramatic descent – *with a good view to the castle and south along the Conwy valley.* After passing further towers the walls level out and you are forced to descend. Go through the wall gap ahead onto the railway station platform. Pass under the road bridge and go up steps, then turn LEFT along Twr Llewelyn. At the junction turn RIGHT back to the start.

WALK 2

CONWY MARINA

DESCRIPTION A 4½ mile walk extending **Walk I** to the Marina and along the sand dunes of Conwy Morfa. Allow about 2½ hours.
START As **Walk I**

C onwy Marina was created from a specially excavated casting basin, where tube sections of Conwy tunnel [1991] were built before being floated into position in the river. Conwy Morfa, a protected area of sand dunes, has an interesting history. During the 19thC people worked here extracting pearls from mussels, and today boats still operate in the estuary, gathering mussels for the table. In 1898 Royal Welsh Fusiliers had a camp here and evidence of their rifle range remains. In 1944 about 900 men worked on the Morfa in great secrecy building sections of the floating harbour, code-named Mulberry, which was used in D-Day landings in Normandy.

I Follow instructions in paragraph **1** of **Walk 1**.

2

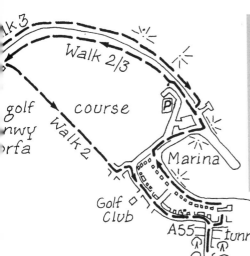

WALK 3

CONWY MORFA

DESCRIPTION A delightful 2 mile walk along the beach at low tide to the marina, returning by a path through the dunes, offering great views. Allow about 1½ hours.

START Conwy Morfa car park [SH 762787] or Marina car park [SH 774790]

DIRECTIONS From junction 17 of the A55 follow signs for the Marina, then for Aberconwy Park to reach the beach car park and toilets.

From the entrance go along the signposted path to an access point onto the beach. Continue beneath the dunes, then rocky foreshore, bending towards the estuary and Deganwy opposite. Just before a

2 Continue past the blue bridge to the entrance to Ysgol Aberconwy and follow the road RIGHT to go over the A55. At Marina Village turn RIGHT to reach The Mulberry (a good refreshment stop) and access to the marina. Continue round the edge of the marina to its far corner by the estuary, then turn LEFT. Go past the top of the slipway and jetty – *enjoying a good view across to Deganwy.* Continue on a path along the edge of the dunes, soon alongside the perimeter fence of the golf course, then bending west above the rocky shoreline. At an old concrete rifle butt turn LEFT to join a nearby stony track. Follow it across the middle of the golf course, then an access road to the nearby road at Marina Village. Follow it to a roundabout and on to join your outward route. Return to point **2**, then follow instructions in paragraph **2** of **Walk 1**. (The next section can easily be varied by following other woodland and parkland paths through Bodlonded as shown, and/or omitting the town walls finale.)

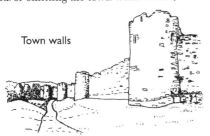

Town walls

jetty go to the top of a slipway, then continue above the beach to the corner of the marina. Return to the slipway then follow a path along the top of the dunes, soon alongside the perimeter fence of the golf course. After passing two old concrete rifle butts the path continues beside the dunes to the start.

WALK 4

CONWY MOUNTAIN (1)

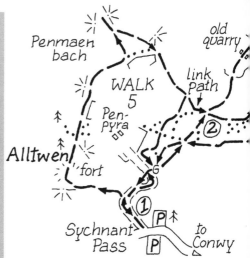

DESCRIPTION A 3¾ mile (**A**) or 3 mile (**B**) walk using the network of delightful paths to explore Conwy Mountain, offering panoramic views. The outward route provides an optional additional ½ mile extension to visit one of its former quarries, before climbing onto its rocky ridge (800 feet/244 metres), with its Iron Age fort. It then descends the superb ridge towards Conwy, before returning on the North Wales Path [NWP] along its lower southern slopes. Allow about 3 hours. The walk can be accessed from Conwy [instructions at the end].

START Top of Sychnant Pass [SH 750770]

DIRECTIONS Follow the one way system west through Conwy past the railway station. After passing under the town walls, turn left up Mount Pleasant. At the T-junction turn right past the youth hostel and follow the road to the top of Sychnant Pass.

1 Take the signposted North Wales Path along a rough lane passing beneath crags and rising, then becoming a stony track. Follow it to a finger post then turn RIGHT with the NWP to a nearby gate. Go up the stony track ahead, shortly descending to a crossroad of green tracks by a waymarker post. Keep ahead to reach another waymarker post – *with a view ahead of the quarried hillside and the Great Orme beyond*. Turn RIGHT. (For the quarry extension follow the path ahead down and across the bracken slope onto the wide grass shelf, then return to the waymarker post.)

2 Go up the NWP, then at another post where the NWP bears right, keep ahead up the stony path, then at a crossroad of paths angle LEFT up the stony path to another path junction. Turn LEFT along the wide path, climbing steadily, soon with a choice of paths onto Conwy Mountain ridge – *offering extensive coastal views.* Go along the higher ridge to pass through Caer Seion hillfort with its stone entrance visible below. *It was used*

between 2300–1900 years ago and contained about 50 round buildings. Shortly the ridge path makes a rocky descent – with a good view down to Conwy castle. An easier option is to follow an adjoining path on the left. The path then levels out – with a view down to Conwy and Deganwy marinas. Shortly it descends again and bends down to the end of a large rock slab.

3 Just before a NWP waymarker post take a wide path leading LEFT. (For Walk B join the returning route at the post.) The path soon descends steadily. At a crossroad of paths either continue down the path or turn LEFT along a small ridge to a metal post overlooking the coast. *Nearby is the remains of a quarry which once produced millstone used for grinding flour.* Turn around and take a path angling LEFT down and across the slope, rising to rejoin the ridge path. Continue down the path, soon by a woodland boundary. At the wall corner the path bends down and round to a ladder-stile above a house, then descends to a road. Follow it RIGHT.

4 Take the signposted NWP up a driveway to a stile. The path rises steadily to reach a waymarker post at a crossroad of paths by the rock slab met earlier. Follow the NWP beneath the rock slab and on up across the southern slopes of Conwy Mountain – *enjoying a good view of Tal-y-fan and the*

4

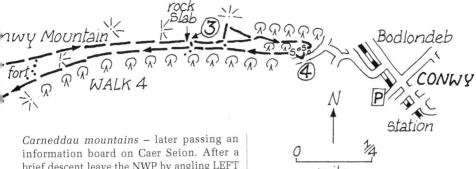

Carneddau mountains – later passing an information board on Caer Seion. After a brief descent leave the NWP by angling LEFT down to join the stony track below near the wall. Follow it to your outward route at the crossroad of tracks. Keep ahead, then take the track's narrow left fork, soon descending to rejoin your outward track again near the gate. At the access track take the signposted NWP over the rise opposite and down to rejoin the track. Follow it back to the start.

Link from Conwy

Follow the one way system past the railway station. After passing under the town walls follow the road ahead, then turn left into Cadnant Park and over the railway line. Go along the road then turn right down Mountain Road and up to a junction. Turn left up the lane to join the walk at point **4**.

WALK 5

ALLTWEN & PENMAEN-BACH

DESCRIPTION An enjoyable 2 mile walk exploring an attractive heather covered Open Access area adjoining Conwy Mountain, featuring two small hills, an Iron Age hillfort, and panoramic views. Allow about 1½ hours. It can easily be linked to Walk 4 to make a great 4¾ mile circuit.

START Top of Sychnant Pass [SH 750770] See **Walk 4**.

Take the signposted North Wales Path along a rough lane passing beneath crags and rising. At a waymarker post opposite a wall corner take a stony path up the heather-covered slope of Alltwen to its summit

for superb all-round mountain and coastal views. Follow a path down its northern side towards a lower top, soon angling RIGHT down to cross the heather-covered ramparts of the hillfort. The path now descends more steeply through heather then gorse to a crossroad of paths in a dip. Follow the path ahead and just beyond a small post take its left fork up to a small rise. Follow the path across the hillside, soon descending and continuing past a wall. Follow the path ahead towards Penmaen-bach – *enjoying extensive coastal views* – soon rising beneath a small crag to reach a wall corner. Take a path on the left up Penmaen-bach to a stone cairn on a ridge overlooking the coast. Retrace your steps then after about 15 yards take another path leading LEFT up over nearby high ground to the hill's small rocky top. Follow the path down to the wall corner – *enjoying a good view of the heavily quarried hillside ahead*. Go ahead alongside the wall then up the green track, soon levelling out then descending.

2 The track then bends right. (To link with Walk 4 angle left down a path to a cross-path below. Follow it left to join the North Wales Path at a nearby waymarker post at point **2** of **Walk 4**.) Follow the track down to a crossroad of paths/tracks. Here follow the track RIGHT towards Alltwen, then take its left fork, over a cross-track, soon bending right and descending. Just before a gate by sheepfolds and the entrance to Pen Pyra turn LEFT to follow the fence to go through a gate at a track. Go to a finger post ahead, then follow the access track back to the start.

WALK 6

CONWY MOUNTAIN (2)

DESCRIPTION A 5¼ mile (**A**) walk with extensive views exploring Conwy Mountain, its Iron Age hillfort, and the attractive varied countryside to its south. After following the North Wales Path to the foot of the hillfort, the walk either climbs through the fort onto the ridge path (route **a**) or continues along the lower NWP North Wales Path (route **b**). The walk returns through Oakwood estate, farmland and upland pasture. Allow about 3½ hours. A 4½ mile (**B**)

START Top of Sychnant Pass [SH 750770]

DIRECTIONS See **Walk 4**.

RIGHT up the path, then continue with the waymarked NWP up and along the southern side of Conwy Mountain to an information board on Caer Seion. (For **route b** simply continue with the NWP.)

2 For **route a** take a path angling up the slope and over a cross path, then turn LEFT into the heart of the hillfort and up through its stone entrance onto the ridge. Follow the path east along the ridge – *enjoying panoramic views* – shortly descending in stages to a crossroad of paths at a NWP waymarker post near a large rock slab. (For **Walk B** follow a path angling right down to a crossroad of paths/tracks at point **3**.) For **Walk A**

I Take the signposted North Wales Path along a rough lane passing beneath crags and rising, becoming a stony track. Later, at a finger post follow the NWP RIGHT to a nearby gate. Go up the stony track ahead, shortly descending to a crossroad of green tracks by a waymarker post. Keep ahead to reach another waymarker post – *with a view ahead of the quarried hillside and the Great Orme beyond.* Turn

turn LEFT and follow the NWP down to a stile, then the driveway of nearby cottages. At the bottom do a sharp U-turn RIGHT along a stony track, shortly rising and becoming a lane. At the gated entrance to Brooklands go through the adjoining gate and up the narrow track alongside a wall. At side paths take the one on the left.

3 Follow the shady path to a kissing gate. Go down a narrow tree/hedged lined stony track to a footbridge over a stream,

6

after which the track rises to a road. Go along Oakwood Lane opposite past houses and Sychnant Pass Nursery. Shortly, turn RIGHT up a driveway past The Mews and nearby Oakwood Park Hall. Follow the road past other estate houses and the access drive to Bryniau, then go through a kissing gate on the left. Go along the wooded field edge, then angle RIGHT to walk near the tree boundary/ stream and on to a gateway in the fence ahead. Go across the next two fields to an access track. Follow the waymarked path ahead to a kissing gate in the right hand corner, then the narrow fenced path to a house. Turn LEFT along the road.

4 At the end of terraced cottages go up a rough access lane on the right. On its bend keep ahead up a wide path to rejoin the lane. Go past Encil-y-coed, then follow its boundary wall round to cross Llechan Uchaf's access track. Follow a path ahead up by the wall, past a small enclosed reservoir, then go up the stony track ahead. Take its left fork, then before a ladder-stile/gate do a sharp U-turn RIGHT to follow a wide green path up through bracken to join the other stony track. At the wall corner turn RIGHT beneath the house and continue along a delightful narrow green track. At a narrow stony cross track follow it RIGHT down to a junction of tracks. Bear LEFT along the stony access track. Soon turn LEFT then follow a wide path past a small shallow reedy lake and go up its left fork to a ladder-stile. Follow the main path along the edge of Pensychnant Nature Reserve to reach the start.

WALK 7
CONWY MOUNTAIN (3)

DESCRIPTION An enjoyable 4 mile anti-clockwise walk of contrasts. From Pensychnant Nature Reserve, the route passes a shallow lake, then heads through Oakwood estate to Conwy Mountain. It then follows an undulating track beneath its lower wooded slopes and visits an attractive area of Open Access land. Allow about 2½ hours.

START Top of Sychnant Pass [SH 750770] or car park beneath Cogwrn [SH 759769]
DIRECTIONS See **Walk 4**.

1 On the south side of the road go through a gate into Pensychnant Nature Reserve. Follow the path alongside the wood past a NWP waymarker post and on to a small covered reservoir, after which the path rises and continues to a ladder-stile. Follow the wide path down and past a shallow reedy lake, then bend LEFT to cross a nearby stony track. Pass beneath the southern end of Cogwrn to a good viewpoint looking towards Conwy Castle and the Little Orme. Turn LEFT, then after a few yards take a narrow path on the right angling down through bracken/gorse to pass a house onto its access track, then follow the road to the car park (the alternative start).

2 Go down the road, then take a path on the right through bracken to a nearby driveway. Go along the access track opposite to Crows Nest Farm, then past cottages. After a gate follow the track's left fork to a ladder-stile, then an enclosed path to the entrance to Inglewood. Go along the road past the access drive to Bryniau, estate houses – *with a good view of Conwy Mountain* – then nearby Oakwood Park Hall, and the Mews. At the T-junction turn LEFT along the narrow road past houses. At a junction. go down a hedge lined track opposite, over a footbridge and up to a kissing gate to enter Conwy Mountain. Go along the path.

3 Shortly, do a sharp U-turn LEFT to follow a track beneath the attractive wooded slope. Shortly the track rises steadily beside a wall, later levelling out. Continue with the undulating track. Later the wall angles away and you reach a waymarker post at a cross-road of tracks. Keep ahead, taking its right fork over two cross tracks, to reach a wall corner. Continue ahead to follow the wall round fields and nearby Pen-pyra, later passing a small shallow lake beneath Alltwen, then follow Pen-pyra's stony access track to Sychnant Pass.

WALK 8

SOUTH OF CONWY

DESCRIPTION A choice of a 5 mile (**A**), 5¼ mile (**B**) or a 3 mile (**C**) walk exploring the attractive undulating countryside south of Conwy, offering good views. Allow about 3½ hours for Walks A & B. The walk can be started from the town centre. From the Visitor Centre head to a nearby tower and follow a cobbled path under the walls. Descend its right fork to pass under the railway line into the car park.
START Car park, Conwy [SH 781774]
DIRECTIONS At the roundabout by the castle take the B5106 (Trefriw) under the castle wall and railway down to enter Gyffin to find the large car park on the right.

I From the car park entrance turn LEFT along the road, then go through a kissing gate on the right. Go up the field to a ladder-stile – *offering a good view of the castle* – then follow a path up through the edge of woodland to a stile and a kissing gate beyond. Go up the field edge past a ladder-stile (your return route) to cross a ladder-stile in the hedge. Angle LEFT to another ladder-stile and a gate beyond. Go across the next field past an old ladder-stile in a former boundary to another in the fence ahead. Go across the field to another ladder-stile, then along the next field edge past the farm onto a road. Follow it LEFT, soon descending past the entrance to Cymnyd Uchaf – *with views into Conwy valley and its tidal river* – then take a signposted path through a gate on the right.

2 Follow a track across the field, then just before an old quarry head LEFT up to a ladder-stile in a fence. Continue to another stile, then go across the next field's mid slopes up to a further stile. These go across the slope of the next field to join a fence boundary. Keep with it as it bends left to go through a kissing gate at a good viewpoint to a finger post beyond. (For **Walk C** turn right along a track and follow it through the caravan site. At a building where it bends left keep ahead to pass through a gap in the

leylandii hedge ahead and on to cross a large metal ladder-stile to a finger post beyond. Turn right up the field edge to a good viewpoint and continue to a finger post. Keep ahead along the next field edge to a kissing gate, then go up the edge of three further fields to a minor road. Follow it left down to point **6**.)

3 Turn LEFT down to another finger post, where you bend RIGHT along a stony track, soon on a meandering descent. When the track splits take the wide right fork past a caravan storage area. After the track bends right take a signposted path on the left, soon bearing RIGHT up to emerge into the caravan site. Take a signposted path LEFT down to a ladder-stile and footbridge to a cross-track. Go past the hedge corner ahead and continue beside it, then follow the path up through trees, past a small building and over a wooden section of fence. Continue with the path through the trees, then alongside the fence and along a field edge beneath chalets – *enjoying a good view across the Conwy valley* – to a ladder-stile. Follow the enclosed path down past a house, then descend its driveway to the B5106. Follow it RIGHT with care.

4 After about 100 yards, go down a road on the left signposted to Henryd. Follow it past Plas Celynin to Henryd. After passing Ysgol Llangelynnin turn RIGHT through the village, soon passing the cemetery. Continue along the attractive country road, later passing a road on the left to reach a cottage. (For **Walk B** go through a kissing gate on the right and up the wide enclosed path. Go past a cottage, then up a field edge to the B5106. Cross the road and follow it left to the entrance to Conwy Touring Park. Go up its access road to a kissing gate on its bend, then follow the path up to rejoin the access road. Follow the signposted wide tree-lined path ahead to a large metal ladder-stile and a finger post beyond where you join **Walk C**).

5 For **Walk A** continue along the road for a further 40 yards then cross a ladder-stile on the right and follow the field edge up to a kissing gate in its top left hand corner. Go

8

round the cottage then up its access lane, soon becoming a stony track, which you follow to the B5106. Take the signposted path along the entry to Cae Cregin opposite to a ladder-stile between the house and the garage. Go up the field to another ladder-stile, then angle LEFT up the next field and follow the boundary down to a ladder-stile. Continue beside the tree boundary to go through a kissing gate, then follow the fence up to a finger post. Turn LEFT and follow the hedge/tree boundary round to a waymarker post. Continue close along the top of a wooded slope down to a finger post at a gap in gorse at a good viewpoint. Here bear RIGHT to another finger post, then descend into the small wooded valley and across the stream to a minor road. Follow it up the hill.

6 Shortly go along a track past the transmitter mast and Bryn Iocyn farm. As it bends into the farmyard go through a kissing gate ahead and on beneath a trig point. Go through a waymarked gateway, soon descending between hedges – *enjoying views across Conwy to the Great Orme* – and continue to a ladder-stile to join your outward route.

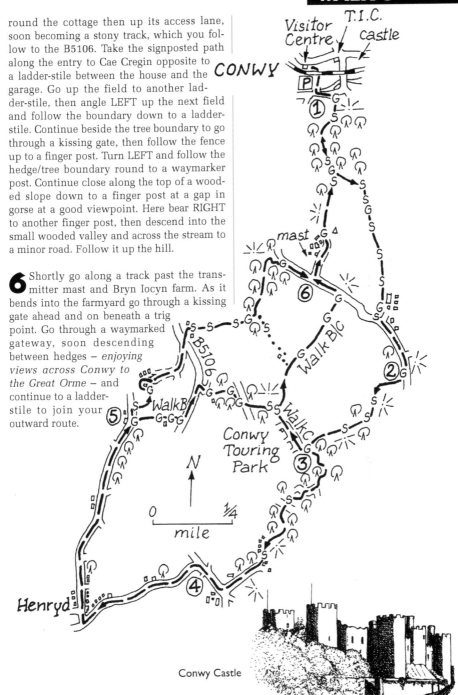

Conwy Castle

ST CELYNIN'S CHURCH

DESCRIPTION A scenic high level 7½ mile walk (**A**) through delightful upland country to one of Snowdonia's remotest ancient churches, offering extensive ever-changing views and featuring two small upland lakes and the remains of a stone circle. The church is reached either by a delightful enclosed bridleway (route **a**) or a hillside viewpoint (route **b**). Allow about 5 hours. Alternative 5 mile (**B**) and 3¾ mile (**C**) walks are included.

START Snowdonia National Park Sychnant car park [SH 755769]

DIRECTIONS The signposted car park lies ⅓ mile east of the top of Sychnant Pass. See **Walk 17**.

*S*t Celynin's *14thC church is an attractive simple building of great character, standing at a junction of several old paths. For centuries it has served this scattered upland community, and despite its remoteness, summer services are still held here at 2pm on the 3rd Sunday in May/July/Sept. In the south corner of the churchyard is a rectangular holy well, which was renowned for its power to heal sick children. Near the churchyard gate once stood an inn which served the many travellers that used to pass by on their journeys across the mountains.*

I Follow the stony track to where it splits. Here bear RIGHT and keep ahead up a narrow stony track through bracken. Shortly, turn LEFT up a narrow green track to a good viewpoint and continue to a house. Go along its access track, then after about 20 yards angle RIGHT to follow a wide green path down to join a stony track to reach a ladder-stile/gate ahead. Continue ahead along the access track to a signposted path junction. Here bear RIGHT past the end of the nearby house. Go along a rough track ahead, then a green track up to a ladder-stile/gate. After another ladder-stile turn LEFT up alongside the fence to a further ladder-stile. Follow

the fence LEFT along the bottom of a wooded slope, soon bending RIGHT and rising, then go across a small field to a ladder-stile. Keep ahead up the next field to pass above oak woodland and descend to a ladder-stile. Cross a farm track below then follow the tree boundary on your right to cross a ladder-stile.

2 Follow the boundary on your right round the edge of a large field to go through a facing gate in the far corner. (For **Walk C** turn right to join a green track above. When it bends left keep ahead alongside the wall to enter a field. Angle left up to a ladder-stile. Follow the path over further ladder-stiles up to a track.) Follow the green track ahead through gates, to reach Hafodty, then turn LEFT down its access track. After ¼ mile, when it bends left, follow a signposted path ahead across tussocky ground to a ladder-stile, then down through trees to a track by outbuildings, Follow it RIGHT past the nearby house, then its access lane up to a road. (For **Walk B** follow it up to its end at point **5**.) Follow the road LEFT down to a junction by Ty'n Lon. Turn RIGHT, signposted to Llangelynnin church. On the bend go through a gate on the left and follow the access lane past outbuildings and a house. Continue up the lane to pass between a cottage and outbuildings. At Cerrig-y-Dinas, go alongside its boundary wall.

3 After a gate at the end of the house you have a choice. For **route a** keep ahead and follow the wall to a gate, then angle LEFT across the field, through a gap in the old boundary, and on across the next field to join the wall. Go past a standing stone and follow the wall to gates in the recessed field corner. Go past Pen-yr-allt. and through a gate. After another gate, turn RIGHT up the enclosed bridleway to the church. For **route b** do a sharp U-turn RIGHT back towards the first cottage, then at a telegraph post angle LEFT across the slope, then up a faint narrow green track. When it bends left, follow a path ahead up the boulder/bracken covered slope. Near the top, the path rises LEFT and continues across the hillside – *with good views north* – soon passing above a wall, then turning LEFT up alongside a fence and continuing to a ladder-stile/gate. Go down the field to a ladder-stile in a wall ahead. Angle LEFT up the field to a gate. Go down a green track and when it bends, keep ahead to pass over a small rise. Just before a ladder-stile, turn LEFT up to another ladder-stile, and on along a track to the church.

4 After leaving the church gate, follow the track RIGHT to cross a ladder-stile on the right and go down the field to another ladder-stile onto a lane. Go up the driveway opposite and on the bend, follow a waymarked path ahead to cross a stream/ladder-stile. Turn LEFT along the field edge to a stile/gate, and through a gate ahead. Go briefly along a stony track, then when it bends left, keep ahead along the field edge to a ladder-stile/gate. Continue ahead to a ladder-stile in the field corner, then along the next long field to a ladder-stile near a cottage. Follow the stiled path across two further fields then alongside a wall to an old iron ladder-stile.

5 Go up to a gate ahead by stone sheepfolds, then up a green track. At a wall corner turn RIGHT to follow another track through reeds and briefly beside the wall. The delightful green track continues across the upland pasture, soon rejoining the wall and passing the remains of a stone circle. Just after a ladder-stile on the right, turn LEFT up a wide green path to join a track which descends a side valley past shallow Llyn y Wrach. At the bottom turn RIGHT along a stony track on the waymarked North Wales Path, which rises steadily. Cross a ladder-stile into Pensychnant Nature Reserve, and follow the North Wales Path on a steady meandering descent to a wood. Here turn RIGHT and follow a path past the wood to a small covered reservoir, after which the path rises and continues to a ladder-stile. Follow the wide path down and past a shallow reedy lake to join your outward route.

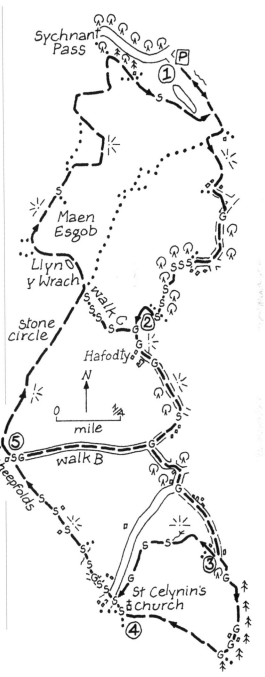

11

TAL-Y-FAN

DESCRIPTION A 8½ mile walk (**A**) for experienced walkers featuring attractive upland country, ancient monuments, a climb to Tal-y-fan (2001 feet/610 metres) and panoramic views throughout. The route follows delightful green tracks up and across upland pasture to Maen Penddu standing stone. It then climbs past an old quarry onto Tal-y-fan and follows a wall along its undulating rocky ridge to its summit trig point. After descending to a bwlch the route returns on good paths across the wild treeless landscape, then across delightful higher ground adjoining the outward route. Allow about 5-6 hours. Avoid in poor visibility. The route can easily be shortened at Maen Penddu, making a less demanding but equally enjoyable alternative 5½ miles (**B**).

START Snowdonia National Park Sychnant car park [SH 755769]

I At the car park entrance go across the track just in front of the barrier and follow a path angling LEFT through bracken, then past the side of the shallow reedy lake to rejoin the track. Follow it to a track junction. Bear RIGHT up the stony track, past another on the left, after which it makes a long steady meandering climb to eventually reach a wall corner, where the track splits. Follow the track ahead briefly near the wall, then down the hillside – *with a good view ahead of Tal-y-fan* – later levelling out and continuing beside the wall past a ladder-stile and the remains of a stone circle. The track then crosses upland pasture – *note a standing stone in field below* – later rejoining the wall. At its next reedy corner follow a path ahead, passing above stone sheepfolds, then continue with a track beside the wall beneath the eastern slopes of Cefn Maen Amor. Shortly when the track splits, go up its right fork. The stony track rises steadily to reach Maen Penddu standing stone. *This flat-topped stone, almost 2 metres high, dates from the 2nd millennium BC and was of likely ceremonial importance.* (For **Walk B** join the returning route here at point **4**.) Continue up the track.

2 When it levels out take the main green track on the left towards the hillside quarry. After passing sheepfolds it becomes a stony track which rises steadily to pass between spoil heaps onto the quarry shelf. Go past two small stone buildings, then bear RIGHT up a green track. After a few yards, just before it bends left, go up a path ahead parallel with the nearby quarry fence to a small stone ruin opposite the fence corner. Now angle RIGHT over a cross-path to follow another path up the hillside, then near the left bank of a stream. When it levels out – *with a view of the wall on the ridge above* – keep ahead, then just beyond where the stream fades into a reedy area follow a path bearing RIGHT which then heads up to join the ridge wall at its corner. Now follow the wall west along the undulating rocky ridge – *enjoying extensive coastal and mountain views* – to a ladder-stile accessing the summit trig point – *a great place to stop to enjoy the all round views*. Recross the ladder-stile and continue west on the ridge path, soon descending then climbing again before beginning a long initially steep descent to a ladder-stile at the bwlch between Tal-y-fan and Foel Lwyd.

3 Here turn RIGHT and follow a path along the edge of a large reedy area, then on a steady descent through heather. Later the path angles LEFT across a short wet reedy area and a stream to join a good path at the end of a rocky knoll. Descend the meandering path, then after about 100 yards it bends half-RIGHT towards a small heather ridge. Keep ahead with the main right fork to go along the bottom of the heather ridge, past a clump of stones to your right – *with a view of a distant coastal windfarm ahead* – and past a path on the left just beyond. Continue along the heather ridge soon bending towards the Great Orme to cross a stream. The path continues across the wild treeless landscape, past stone sheepfolds, after which it steadily descends. When reservoirs in the valley below come into view the path bends eastwards, passes through a wet reedy area and crosses streams. After passing an unusual stone shelter (*possibly a peathouse*) continue along an old green track, soon rising steadily to join your outward route at point **2**.

4 At Maen Penddu take a path on the left. After about 60 yards take its right fork, then follow the clear path across bilberry/gorse covered Cefn Maen Amor – *with a view of the Great Orme ahead* – to reach the large erratic boulders of Maen Amor. Follow the path down its northern slope to a faint green cross-track. Keep ahead to join a green track angling left, soon being joined by another. Follow it towards the Little Orme. When the faint track bends right follow a path ahead through gorse to join your outward track near the wall. Now take a wide green path angling LEFT up and across the wide gorse/heather covered top of Waen Gyrach – *enjoying panoramic all round views, and soon your next path rising across Maen Esgob ahead* – then descending. Just before it levels out take its left fork then follow a path up the small slope opposite and follow a path LEFT up to a small stone cairn on the summit of Maen Esgob. Follow a path angling RIGHT down to join a track by a small shallow pool and follow it RIGHT to rejoin your outward track. Descend the track. Later at a view down to Cogwrn take a path on the left angling down through bracken. Keep down its left fork to join the track in the valley. Follow it beneath Cogwrn back to the start

Cogwrn

lake

①

pool

Maen Esgob

Maen Gyrach

N

0   ¼

mile

stone circle

Cefn Maen Amor

Maen Amor

② ④

walk 21

quarry

Maen Penddu

Tal-y-Fan

S

A

③

Maen Penddu

13

AROUND SYCHNANT PASS

DESCRIPTION An exhilarating 3½ mile walk exploring the hills around Sychnant Pass, offering great views. Starting at the top of the Pass the route passes a small upland lake, then after a short steep descent, continues down through attractive woodland to Dwygyfylchi and on to Capelulo, with its choice of old inns. It then climbs above a side valley and returns along a high-level scenic path above the Sychnant Pass. Allow about 3 hours.

START Top of Sychnant Pass [SH 750770]
DIRECTIONS See **Walk 4**.

1 Take the signposted North Wales Path along a rough lane, soon rising towards Alltwen and becoming a stony track. Continue along the track and later as it approaches the gated entrance to Penprya, angle LEFT to follow a path past a wall corner. Continue beside the wall and pass either side of a small shallow lake. The path then rises and splits. Keep straight ahead, then after about 25 yards, with a wall corner ahead, take its left fork to a small rise offering extensive coastal views. At a cross-path just beyond follow it LEFT, soon descending past a small wooden post to a path junction. Turn RIGHT.

2 Follow the path down towards the nearby wood corner, then descend the steep slope by the wood edge. At a level crosspath, follow it LEFT through bracken down to a ladder-stile/gate. The path now descends through Coed Pendryffryn. After about 100 yards, leave the main woodland path to take an indistinct path on the left angling across a small exposed stony bank up to a fence. The narrow path continues beside the fence beneath the scree slopes of Alltwen, past a ladder-stile, then on through the top of the wood just below the boundary. The path soon descends steadily, passing two waymarker posts to join a wide path, which you follow to a kissing gate. Continue down the path to pass the rear, then the front of a row of terrace houses to cross a bridge over the river to Old Mill Road in Dwygyfylchi. Follow the road LEFT alongside the river. Shortly, take a signposted path along the access track to Y Glyn. The path continues briefly beside the river and through trees to Conwy Old road opposite Y Dwygyfylchi and nearby Fairy Glen inn in Capelulo. Go up the road opposite, past toilets and the village hall to a Snowdonia National Park sign.

3 Take a signposted path across a bridge on the left and follow the driveway to the gated entrance to a house. Take the signposted path on a steady climb up the bracken-covered hillside to reach a wall corner. (An alternative return [**B**] is to follow the path ahead up between walls, then on past nearby Penfforddgoch. At a gate in the wall turn left up a green track to join another above – the North Wales Path/**Walk 12**). Turn LEFT and follow a narrow path up across the steep hillside. After briefly descending it continues across the steep heather/bracken covered slope to a small rocky top, then descends to a seat at a good viewpoint overlooking Sychnant Pass and continues down to the start.

ALLTWEN & CWM GYRACH

DESCRIPTION A 5½ mile walk exploring the upland area around Capelulo, with ever-changing views. After a climb up Alltwen with its Iron Age hillfort the route descends steeply, then continues down through attractive woodland to Dwygyfylchi, and on to nearby Capelulo, with its choice of old inns. It then climbs steadily on delightful green tracks into open hill country to make a high-level circuit of the Gyrach valley, returning along the waymarked North Wales Path. Allow about 4 hours.

START Top of Sychnant Pass [SH 750770]
DIRECTIONS See **Walk 4**.

WALK 11 & 12

1 Take the signposted North Wales Path along a rough lane, soon rising towards Alltwen and becoming a stony track. At a waymarker post opposite a wall corner take a stony path up the heather-covered slope to Alltwen's summit for superb all-round views. Follow a path down its northern side, soon crossing the ramparts of the hillfort, and descending more steeply through heather then gorse to a crossroad of paths in a dip.

2 Follow instructions in paragraph **2** of **Walk 11**.

3 Continue ahead along the road past cottages, after which it rises steadily, then levels out and becomes two tracks. Here do a sharp U-turn up to a nearby gate. Follow the track up the edge of woodland and on to a signposted path junction above a cottage at a prominent viewpoint. Continue with the delightful green track as it meanders up the hillside past another finger post. It continues rising steadily into attractive open country soon alongside a wall on your left. Eventually it levels out and splits. Continue near the wall, soon being joined by another green track, and passing an iron ladder-stile. Shortly the track bends RIGHT and is joined by another track from a nearby chalet. Keep with its left fork to pass Tyn-ffridd farm.

4 Just beyond its boundary corner turn LEFT up a green track and on to a path junction. Turn LEFT to cross the nearby ladder-stile and follow the path LEFT to join the North Wales Path at a waymarker post. Follow the path to a ladder-stile and a footbridge over the Afon Gyrach – a delightful place for a break. Continue with the path to pass a wall corner. At a waymarker post by the wall near a ruin, turn LEFT to follow the NWP across open country and down to join a wall. At its next corner the NWP becomes a green track which descends to pass a side valley, then rises steadily. When it bends right cross a ladder-stile ahead into Pensychnant Nature Reserve and follow the meandering NWP down to a path junction at a wood, then LEFT to a gate at the start.

Sychnant Pass is the most northerly pass in Snowdonia National Park. The road through it was built in the 18thC as part of the mail coach route. Inns opened at Capelulo, which became an important coaching stop for travellers until a new coastal road was opened in the 1820s. Despite loss of the passing trade, it became a popular place for Victorian visitors who enjoyed horse-drawn trips.

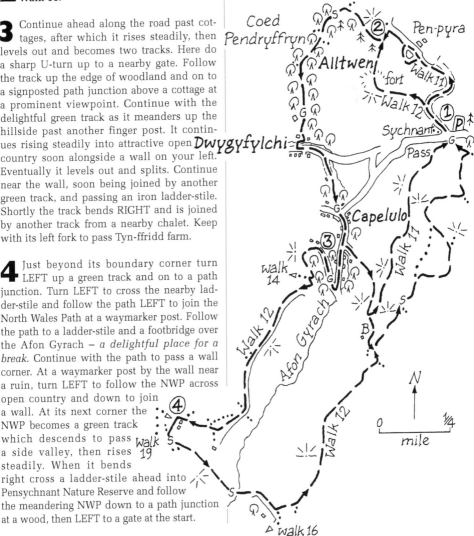

15

SYCHNANT PASS

DESCRIPTION A short but impressive 2 mile walk following a path across steep slopes above Sychnant Pass offering good views, then descending to Capelulo, with its two country inns, before returning up the historic Pass (See **Walk 12** for details.) Allow about 2 hours.
START Top of Sychnant Pass [SH 750770]
DIRECTIONS See **Walk 4**.

I On the south side of the road just before a gate giving access to Pensychnant Nature Reserve, turn RIGHT along a path passing above the car parking area. It rises steadily to a seat at a good viewpoint, then continues up the hillside to a small rocky top offering new views. It now contours across the steep heather/bracken slope, briefly climbs again, then gradually descends. Visible below is your next path. At a wall corner turn RIGHT and follow a path down the bracken covered hillside above the wooded valley to the gated entrance to a house. Follow its driveway to cross over the river to reach a minor road.

2 Follow it RIGHT past the Village Hall to the main road in Capelulo. Go through a small iron gate opposite Y Dwygyfylchi and follow the signposted path past a children's play area and woodland, then along Y Glyn's access track to a road. Turn RIGHT up the road beneath the steep slopes of Alltwen. On the bend go up the rough no through road ahead by Llys Gwynt. After passing other houses a path rises steadily beneath the craggy slopes of Alltwen to the top of the pass.

FOEL LUS

DESCRIPTION An exhilarating 6½ mile (**A**) walk exploring the dramatic upland landscape around Capelulo, featuring the heather covered hill of Foel Lus (1188 feet/362 metes), with panoramic views throughout. The route crosses steep slopes above Sychnant Pass and Capelulo, then descends into wooded Cwm Cyrach, after which it climbs towards Foel Lus.

After a climb to its top or a lower alternative it then follows Jubilee Walk, a breathtaking high level path around Foel Lus created to celebrate Queen Victoria's Jubilee in 1887. Afterwards it descends its eastern slope, then passes through attractive woodland to reach Capelulo. From nearby Dwygyfylchi the route climbs through Coed Pendryffryn and across open slopes, before returning by path and track. Allow about 4 hours. The route can easily be shortened to a 5 mile walk (**B**).
START Top of Sychnant Pass [SH 750770]

I Follow instructions in paragraph **1** of **Walk 13**.

2 Follow it LEFT up past cottages to where the road levels out and becomes two tracks. Here do a sharp U-turn up to a nearby gate. Follow the track up to a signposted path junction above a cottage at a prominent viewpoint. Continue up the delightful meandering green track. At another finger post take a path angling back on the right towards Foel Lus across the steep heather/bracken hillside, soon passing above a deep side valley. At its top cross a stream and just beyond bear RIGHT to follow a wide green path up past a small tree and on to join a level green path beneath pylons. Follow it ahead to a nearby seat by a telegraph pole at a junction of paths – *a good place to stop to enjoy the views*. (For **Walk B** return down to point **5**.)

3 Turn sharp LEFT up the path to a telegraph pole. Here you have a choice. **Route a**: take a stony path on the right up the eastern slope of Foel Lus to its summit – *offering all round views*. After visiting a nearby lower top for enhanced coastal views return to follow a stony path down its southern slope, later becoming a rough track and passing a path on the right. At a cross path just before the bend of a track ahead at point **4**, turn RIGHT. **Route b**: continue up the path to join an access track, which you follow ahead, soon rising past a side track. Just before it bends left turn RIGHT up a path towards Foel Lus for about 10 yards to a cross-path where you join the descending summit heather track. Turn LEFT.

4 Follow the path down through heather – *with a good view down to Penmaenmawr and Anglesey* – to a stony track. Follow it RIGHT, soon descending. On its bend go between the two stone columns, the 'gateway' to the Jubilee Path. Follow the wide stony path – *enjoying stunning changing coastal views* – across the steep scree-covered slopes. Later the path bends inland to reach the seat at point **3**. Return along your outward route, soon descending past the small tree towards the side valley.

5 Now follow a clear path leading back towards the Great Orme across the top of the valley, then descending to a grassy area in a dip.

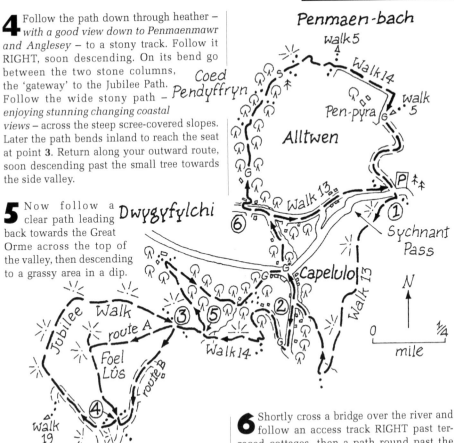

Here turn RIGHT a few yards, then follow a clear path angling down the hillside towards Dwygyfylchi to reach a wall corner amongst trees. Continue down beside the boundary to a finger post above houses. Here do a sharp U-turn RIGHT and follow a good path across the attractive wooded slope. After crossing a stream above a large house the path splits. Follow the one LEFT past the house, through trees and down past a finger post to a kissing gate onto the road in Capelulo. Follow it RIGHT then go through a small iron gate opposite Y Dwygyfylchi. Follow the path past a children's play area and woodland, then along Y Glyn's access track to a road. Follow it LEFT into Dwygyfylchi.

6 Shortly cross a bridge over the river and follow an access track RIGHT past terraced cottages, then a path round past the rear of the cottages and up to a kissing gate to enter Coed Pendryffryn. Go along the wide woodland path, then take a narrow way-marked path on the right. It rises steadily along the wood edge, later passing a ladder-stile beneath the scree slopes of Alltwen, to join a wide woodland path. Follow it up to a ladder-stile then up through bracken. After about 40 yards, where a path rises right along the wood edge, follow a path ahead rising across the bracken/rhododendron slope towards Penmaen-bach, keeping with its upper right fork. Just before a scree slope the path begins a steady zig zag up the hillside. At the top go to a wall corner ahead and continue alongside the wall. At its corner turn RIGHT and follow a path beside it down to a gate beyond sheepfolds onto Pen-prya's access track. Follow it back to the start.

WALK 15

ABOVE SYCHNANT PASS

DESCRIPTION A choice of two short walks exploring the attractive upland area near the Sychnant Pass, enjoying good views. The 2½ mile walk (**A**) features a small shallow pool and a reedy lake. The 2 mile walk (**B**) visits a hilltop memorial. Allow about 1½–2 hours.
START Top of Sychnant Pass [SH 750770]
DIRECTIONS See **Walk 4**.

1 On the south side of the road go through a gate into Pensychnant Nature Reserve and follow the path alongside the wood then do a sharp U-turn RIGHT and continue up the waymarked North Wales Path (NWP)/ bridleway, which rises steadily in stages up the bracken covered hillside – *offering good views*. When it splits go up the waymarked bridleway to rejoin the NWP at another waymarker post. First turn RIGHT along a rough path to a small rock top offering panoramic views, then return to the waymarker post.

2 For **Walk A** continue ahead on the NWP, soon descending to a ladder-stile/gate at a good viewpoint. Turn LEFT up the stony track, later levelling out and passing a small shallow pool to join a cross-track near a wall corner. Follow the stony track on a long steady meandering descent to eventually level out at a junction of tracks. Follow the stony track LEFT. Soon take a path on the left then continue past a small shallow reedy lake, and go up the path's left fork to a ladder-stile. Follow the path down to a small covered reservoir and along the edge of a wood to the start. For **Walk B** turn LEFT along the NWP, soon descending steadily. Just before it bends left down to a waymarker post head RIGHT across rough upland pasture to the wall. Follow a path down beside the wall then up onto a small ridge offering a good view of Conwy Castle. Follow a narrow path LEFT to a memorial cairn to Muriel Nevill Tattersall. Now follow a path leading LEFT, soon descending to a rocky outcrop. The path bends down LEFT and continues

round beneath the crag, from which a path descends through bracken then heather and across a small ridge to rejoin the NWP.

WALK 16

UPLAND RESERVOIRS

DESCRIPTION An undulating 5 mile (**A**) walk exploring the attractive upland landscape south of the Sychnant Pass. The route follows the scenic North Wales Path up into wilder upland country, then Walk A continues to two remote upland reservoirs. The return follows delightful green tracks, passing the remains of a stone circle and a shallow lake before an exhilarating finale following a path across the steep hillside above Sychnant Pass. Allow about 3½ hours. The route includes alternative 3¾ mile (**B**) and 2 mile (**C**) walks.
START Top of Sychnant Pass [SH 750770]
DIRECTIONS See **Walk 4**.

1 On the south side of the road go through a gate into Pensychnant Nature Reserve and follow the path alongside the wood then do a sharp U-turn RIGHT and continue up the waymarked NWP/bridleway, which rises steadily in stages up the bracken covered hillside – *offering good views*. When it splits continue up either the NWP or the bridleway.

2 When they meet again keep ahead on the NWP, soon descending to a ladder-stile/gate at a good viewpoint. The NWP continues down a stony track, shortly bending to a waymarker post at a side valley, where you meet your return route. (For **Walk C** turn right and resume text at point **6**.) Continue with the NWP up the track to join a wall, where it becomes a path. Shortly, the NWP moves away from the wall and rises across upland pasture towards Tal-y-fan. Later it levels out and continues past a large boulder then a faint track on the left, where it bends up to reach a waymarker post at a facing wall. Here you leave the NWP by turning LEFT up near the wall.

18

3 At its corner turn RIGHT. (For **Walk B** continue ahead up a faint green track, soon levelling out. Keep ahead soon descending to point **5**.) At the next corner keep ahead along a green track, shortly being joined by another from the left. Keep ahead, angling LEFT with the track. After about 80 yards you pass a path angling up to a green track above to reach a small crossroad of paths at the edge of an area of gorse. Take the RIGHT fork through the gorse towards the top of a line of distant telegraph poles. After crossing streams take the path's LEFT fork to pass through more gorse to reach stone sheepfolds above the Afon Gyrach.

4 Work your way round the sheepfolds then along the gorse covered bank of the river and up an adjoining reedy hollow. After rejoining the river climb onto the dam of a hidden reservoir. Turn LEFT across the dam then along the side of the reservoir to a second lilly covered reservoir – *a great place to stop.* Return to the dam corner of the first reservoir then turn sharp RIGHT up a green track. Follow it across heather terrain to join a green cross-track. Follow it beneath the

slopes of Cefn Maen Amor towards the Great Orme, shortly crossing higher ground – *with a view down to the wall corner at point* **3** – then descending to a crossroad of green tracks/paths. Turn RIGHT and follow the path across a small wet area, soon descending a green track.

5 Just before a reedy wall corner turn LEFT and follow a track between the reeds, briefly beside the wall, then across open pasture soon rejoining the wall. Shortly the green track passes the remains of a stone circle. Just after a ladder-stile on the right, turn LEFT along a path to join a track which descends a side valley past shallow Llyn y Wrach (may be dry) to a NWP waymarker post at your outward route.

6 Keep ahead to join the wall below. Follow it RIGHT, over a track and down past nearby Penfforddgoch, then briefly between walls. At the wall corner overlooking a side valley leading to Capelulo the path splits. Take the path bearing RIGHT and rising across the steep hillside. After briefly descending it continues across the steep heather/bracken covered slope to a small rocky top, then descends to a seat at a good viewpoint overlooking Sychnant Pass, before continuing down to the start.

WALK 17

MAEN ESGOB

DESCRIPTION A 4 mile (**A**) or 2¾ mile (**B**) walk using the network of delightful paths and tracks to explore attractive upland country, featuring several low hills offering panoramic views. The route first climbs nearby Cogwrn then meanders into open country to visit the small top of Maen Esgob (984 feet/300 metres). Walk A continues across Waen Gyrach, before returning to join Walk B for a visit to the small crag of Craigyfedwen. Allow about 2½ hours.

START Snowdonia National Park Sychnant car park [SH 755769]

DIRECTIONS Follow the one way system west through Conwy past the railway station. After passing under the town walls, turn left up Mount Pleasant. At the T-junction turn right past the youth hostel. Continue along the road, past a road and car park on the left, and up past the entrance to Pensychnant Nature Conservation Centre to find the signposted car park along a lane on the left.

I From the north eastern corner of the car park take a path up to the top of Cogwrn, then walk along its small ridge and down its southern slope to join the nearby stony track. Follow it up to a track junction, then take the left fork down to the entrance to a cottage. Continue down a path to join a road by Ty Coch farm. Go along the road then at the end of terraced cottages take a signposted path up a rough access lane on the right. On its bend keep ahead up a wide path to rejoin the lane. Go past Encil-y-coed, then turn LEFT across the access track to Llechan Uchaf and follow a path up by the wall past a small enclosed reservoir. Go up the stony track ahead, keeping to its right fork, soon alongside a wall. At its corner just below a large house keep ahead to follow a green track up the bracken covered hillside to join a cross-track near a wall corner.

2 Follow it LEFT then after a few yards take its right fork, soon passing a small shallow pool. Just beyond take a path on the left up the heather covered slopes of Maen

Esgob to a small stone cairn on its top. (For **Walk B** take the alternative path back down to the track and join the wall beyond, then follow instructions from paragraph **6** of **Walk 18**.) For **Walk A** follow a delightful path down its southern slopes, soon passing above a side valley containing the shallow lake of Llyn y Wrach. Take the second path on the right down to a crossroad of paths in a hollow. Keep ahead through gorse then follow a wide path angling RIGHT up the hillside and across the wide heather/gorse top of Waen Gyrach towards Tal-y-fan, later angling down to join a green track near a wall.

3 Here turn sharp LEFT and follow the track back to point **2** near the wall corner. Keep ahead down the track then on the bend take the path angling RIGHT, then another path leading RIGHT to the small rocky top of Craigyfedwen. Take a nearby path down to rejoin the track. Follow it down to join your outward route, then follow either the lakeside path or the track back to the start.

WALK 18

MAEN PENDDU

DESCRIPTION A 7¼ mile upland walk (**A**) which extends Walk 17A to visit several of the area's interesting features. After Waen Gyrach the route climbs onto Cefn Maen Amor to visit large erratic boulders (1286 feet/392 metres). After visiting Maen Penddu standing stone, the route returns by a delightful green track, visits nearby upland reservoirs (optional), then follows a section of the North Wales Path, before rejoining Walk 17 for a final view from Craigyfedwen. Allow about 5 hours. The route includes an alternative 5 mile walk (**B**).

START As **Walk 17**.

I-2 Follow instructions in paragraphs 1-2 of **Walk 17A**.

3 Keep ahead along the track then after a few yards follow a path angling RIGHT up through gorse. Soon continue on a green track ahead to where it splits. (For **Walk B** take its right fork to a crossroad of paths/

tracks. Turn right to join the returning route at point **5**.) For **Walk A** take its left fork, then when it bends left keep ahead to cross a green track and follow a clear path ahead up the gorse/heather slopes of Cefn Maen Amor to reach large erratic boulders know as Maen Amor. Continue with the path across the bilberry/heather terrain. Later take its left fork towards the quarry on Tal-y-fan and on towards Maen Penddu standing stone now visible. *This flat-topped stone, almost 2 metres high, and an almost buried stone circle nearby, date from the 2nd millennium BC and were of likely ceremonial importance.* Turn RIGHT up the part stony track, soon levelling out and passing a track leading to the hillside quarry. Soon the green track descends towards an expansive wide valley.

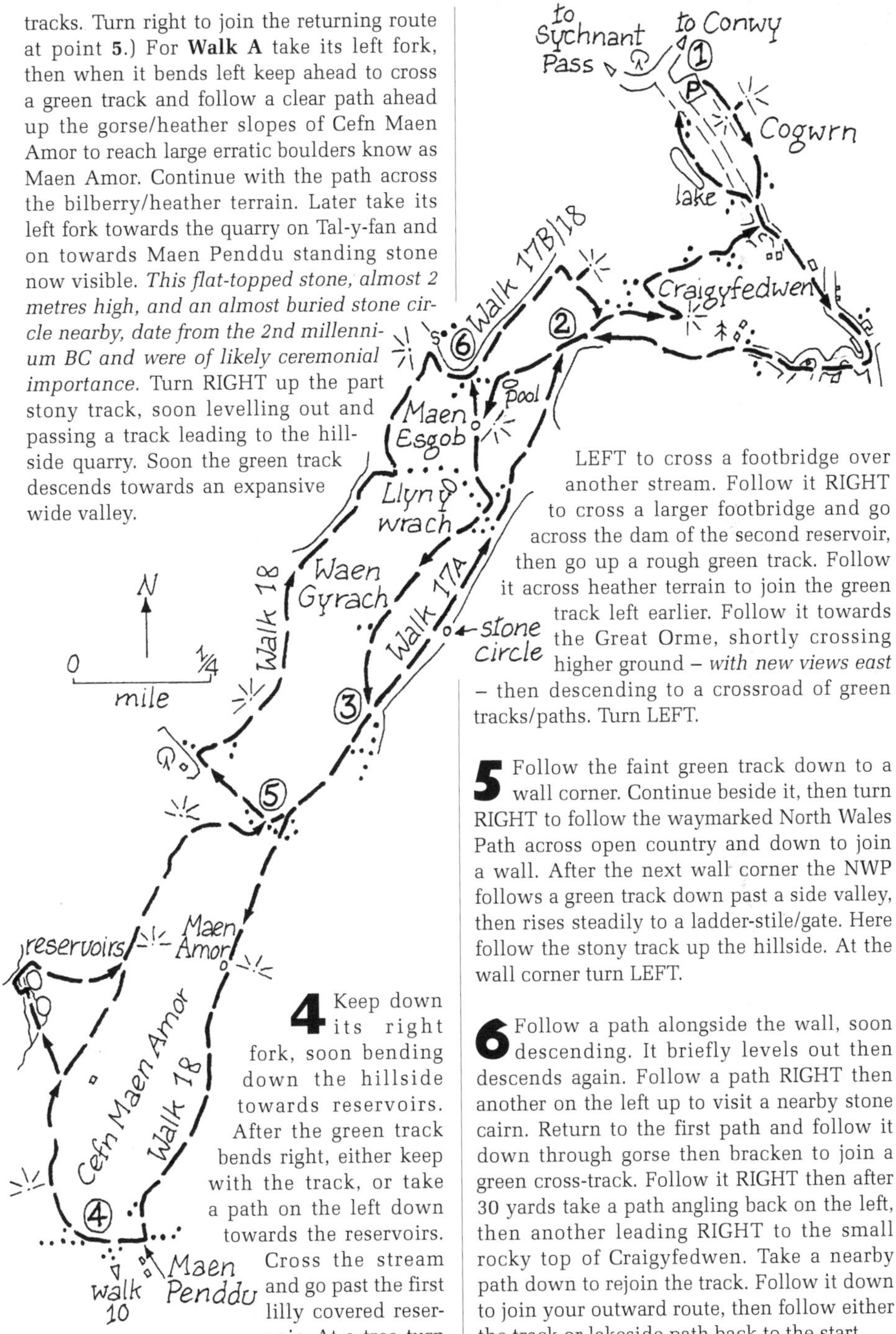

LEFT to cross a footbridge over another stream. Follow it RIGHT to cross a larger footbridge and go across the dam of the second reservoir, then go up a rough green track. Follow it across heather terrain to join the green track left earlier. Follow it towards the Great Orme, shortly crossing higher ground – *with new views east* – then descending to a crossroad of green tracks/paths. Turn LEFT.

5 Follow the faint green track down to a wall corner. Continue beside it, then turn RIGHT to follow the waymarked North Wales Path across open country and down to join a wall. After the next wall corner the NWP follows a green track down past a side valley, then rises steadily to a ladder-stile/gate. Here follow the stony track up the hillside. At the wall corner turn LEFT.

4 Keep down its right fork, soon bending down the hillside towards reservoirs. After the green track bends right, either keep with the track, or take a path on the left down towards the reservoirs. Cross the stream and go past the first lilly covered reservoir. At a tree turn

6 Follow a path alongside the wall, soon descending. It briefly levels out then descends again. Follow a path RIGHT then another on the left up to visit a nearby stone cairn. Return to the first path and follow it down through gorse then bracken to join a green cross-track. Follow it RIGHT then after 30 yards take a path angling back on the left, then another leading RIGHT to the small rocky top of Craigyfedwen. Take a nearby path down to rejoin the track. Follow it down to join your outward route, then follow either the track or lakeside path back to the start.

(Map labels: to Sychnant Pass, to Conwy, Cogwrn, lake, Craigyfedwen, Walk 17B/18, Pool, Maen Esgob, Llyn wrach, Waen Gyrach, Walk 18, Walk 17A, stone circle, N, 0 ¼ mile, reservoirs, Maen Amor, Cefn Maen Amor, Walk 18, Maen Penddu, walk 10)

DRUIDS CIRCLE & FOEL LUS

DESCRIPTION A 5¼ mile (**A**) or 4¼ mile (**B**) walk exploring the attractive hills and upland plateau above Penmaenmawr, featuring the famous Bronze Age Druids Circle, other ancient groups of stones, and superb views. **Walk A** includes an exhilarating high level panoramic walk around Foel Lus created to celebrate Queen Victoria's Jubilee in 1887. There is also an option to climb to the top of Foel Lus (1188 feet/362 metres). After the initial steep ascent to reach the Circle standing at just over 1300 feet/400 metres, the rest of the route offers delightful walking. Allow about 3½ hours.

START Car park by the library, Penmaenmawr [SH 719763].

DIRECTIONS At crossroads in the centre of Penmaenmawr go up Fernbrook road, signposted to the library to find a large car park on the right. This walk is also accessible by bus or train.

The hill and upland plateau above Penmaenmawr are rich in archaeological evidence of early man. On the hill that towers above the town to the south, heavily scarred by quarrying for granite, which continues to this day, is the site of Graiglwyd Neolithic axe factory – the third largest production centre in Britain. Stone stronger than flint was first removed in blocks, then pieces flaked by hammerstone into rough shape, before being polished and attached to wooden handles. As Neolithic man began to settle on the land, axes were needed for clearing dense forest to create pasture, and building wooden houses. Axes made here have been found throughout Britain, indicating the existence of an extensive trading network. Later, partly encouraged by an improvement in climate, early Bronze Age man moved into the uplands, leaving behind an extensive range of burial and ritual monuments.

I From the car park, turn RIGHT up the road and just past Y Berllan, go up a railed stepped pathway on the right. At its top turn RIGHT along a lane past houses, and at a road junction, turn LEFT. After a few yards, bear RIGHT on a tarmaced path past the end of Llys Machno up to a road. Go up the road to a kissing gate ahead. Go up the tree-lined path to a gate by a ruin and on up a field to a kissing-gate onto a road. Follow it LEFT, then turn RIGHT up a driveway on a signposted path. Follow the waymarked path to the left of buildings, past a corner wall and up to a kissing gate. Now follow the delightful green path up the hillside, soon near a fence past a small wood. At the fence corner keep with the main path rising steadily up the edge of an attractive side valley. A bench seat and excellent views looking back assist in the increasingly steep climb. *Nearby to the west is the heavily quarried Graiglwyd mountain and site of the Neolithic axe factory.* After another bench seat the path crosses a low concrete footbridge across a stream and a reedy area, then rises to a kissing gate in the wall ahead. Go up the slope ahead to join the North Wales Path at a waymarker post. Turn RIGHT and follow the path west near the wall to reach a narrow track by a waymarker post.

2 Here, turn LEFT along the green track – *past the scant remains of a stone circle* – which quickly becomes a path. Keep to its higher right fork to unexpectedly reach a more substantial stone circle on the edge of a plateau leading to Tal y Fan and grazed by wild ponies. A little further on is the Druids Circle – *an impressive large embanked stone circle dating from the 2nd millennium BC which, in the 18thC was often sketched by travellers who passed by on the ancient mountain road below. It was probably originally used for rituals, then later for burials, as evidenced by the cremated remains of several young children found in its centre.* Descend across a gully and follow the clear path down and along to join the North Wales Path at a waymarker post. Just to your right is the remains of another small stone circle.

3 Continue with the North Wales Path, soon near a wall – *enjoying extensive coastal views from Llandudno to Rhyl.* After going through a kissing gate in the wall the path descends then bears LEFT along a tree-

to A55

library

PENMAENMAWR

Foel Lûs

fishery

walk B

N

0   ¼
mile

Maen
Crwn

Druids
Circle

walk 20

Walk 12

lined green track to pass Bryn Derwydd. *Nearby is Maen Crwn, a large glacial erratic stone.* After a gate continue along the track. *In the field to your right are several small stones – the remains of a stone circle.* When the North Wales Path goes through a gate on the right, continue along the track to a kissing gate/gate and on to join another track coming in from the right. Keep ahead.

4 Go past another track on the right (another option – you join it shortly), then a seat and a stone route marker, after which the track descends – *offering dramatic views over Penmaenmawr and across to Anglesey.* (For **Walk B** either descend the steep slope on the left to a kissing gate or continue down the track to point **5.**) Just beyond the bend where the track levels out take a path angling back on the right up the heather slope. Keep to its right fork (the left fork offers an optional climb

to the top of Foel Lus) to join the stony track. Follow it LEFT, soon descending past side tracks and continuing alongside a wall. At the wall corner, when the track bends down to a house, continue straight ahead on a path through heather, soon descending past telegraph poles – *with a superb view towards the Great Orme, Conwy Mountain, and Sychnant Pass.* At a junction of paths, bear LEFT past a seat to follow the higher Jubilee Path contouring around the steep slopes of Foel Lus – *enjoying breathtaking coastal views.*

5 After passing through the 'gateway' to the Jubilee Path – go down the road. Later, go through a kissing gate on the left opposite an underground reservoir. Go along the field edge passing above a farm, later joining its access track, then cross a ladder-stile on the right. Follow the fenced path round the edge of the fishery and past the caravan site to a kissing gate, then continue down a lane. At a road junction, turn LEFT, and after a few yards RIGHT to follow an enclosed path to join your outward route by Llys Machno.

23

CLIP YR ORSEDD

DESCRIPTION A 6¼ mile walk (**A**) exploring the hills east of Llanfairfechan, offering extensive views. The walk rises in stages to reach wild upland pasture grazed by wild ponies, then either continues along the small ridge of Clip yr Orsedd (1407 feet/429 metres) [**route a**] or skirts its lower southern slopes [**route b**]. It then follows the waymarked North Wales Path on a long steady descent back towards Llanfairfechan. Allow about 4 hours. The route includes a shorter 3¾ mile walk (**B**) and can easily be extended to visit the Druids Circle, ⅓ mile beyond point **4**.

START Llanfairfechan [SH 682747]

DIRECTIONS Turn off the A55 into Llanfairfechan. At traffic lights by shops turn up Village Road. Go past the Co-op, then turn right between the HSBC bank and the school to a small car park behind the bank.

*T*he **area** around Llanfairfechan has been occupied by man since early times, but it was not until the mid-19thC with the arrival of the railway that it developed into a popular tourist resort.

I Return to the main road and turn LEFT, then just beyond the Co-op go along Park Road opposite, passing side roads, the Church Institute and modern houses/bungalows. When the road bends right, go through the iron gates of Penmaen Park ahead. Go along the stony track, following its right fork – *enjoying fine views across to Anglesey and Puffin Island* – up to a gate at its end. Continue along a road past houses. When it bends left by Bryn Goleu go up a stony track passing beneath a large house.

2 At its boundary wall corner turn RIGHT to a kissing gate to enter Tyddyn Drycin. Go up through the wood. Soon, at a crossroad of paths, turn RIGHT and follow the path up through the wood. At a waymarked path junction, turn RIGHT to a kissing gate. The enclosed path now rises steadily to reach a small gate, then continues up behind houses,

past a waymarked path on the right. Just beyond, and below a kissing gate, bend LEFT with the path – *enjoying great views across to Anglesey* – up to another kissing gate. Follow the path up through trees, after which it rises steadily across the open hillside – *offering superb views along the coast and inland to the mountains* – to eventually reach a kissing gate by a clump of trees. Continue beside the wall – *enjoying fine views to Tal-y-fan ahead, and across towards Drum* – to its corner by Scots Pines and a nearby quarry road. (For **Walk B** turn right and follow the wall down past sheds by the bend of the quarry road, and on down to a kissing gate. Continue down past the end of a wood, over a stile by a cottage. Follow the wall down through the trees to a gate by the entrance to Newry Cottage and on to the road below. Turn right and resume instructions from the relevant point in paragraph **4**.)

3 Continue ahead alongside another wall, soon joining the quarry road, which rises steadily. On its bend go through a kissing gate ahead and follow the fence, then wall on your right across wild upland country towards the small rocky end of Clip yr Orsedd. Shortly you have a choice. For **route a** just before a telegraph pole angle away from the wall across open ground for a short climb on to the rocky western top of Clip

road. The track soon begins a steady descent. After a gate the path continues down beside a fence – *with a good view along the coast and across to Anglesey* – passes through another gate, and continues down to a cottage. Go along its access track past farm buildings. After a gate by a descending quarry road, keep ahead down the road to Newry Cottage, where you are joined by **Walk B**.

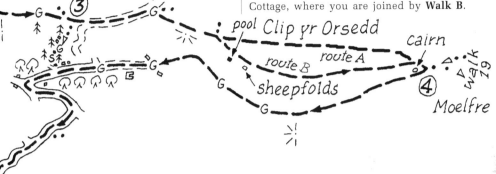

yr Orsedd for panoramic all-round views. Follow a path along the wide ridge to its small eastern rocky top, then descend to a wall corner. Continue to the telegraph pole ahead, then follow a path past two further poles and down parallel with a wall to point **4** at a collapsed stone-topped cairn. For **route b** keep alongside the wall to pass a small part wall-enclosed rectangular pool. At sheepfolds, follow the rising track angling away from the wall, soon levelling out. Continue past the southern slopes of Clip yr Orsedd, then beneath a line of telegraph poles to pass a cairn.

4 At a nearby green track below, by a reedy area beneath the flat-topped small hill of Moelfre you join the North Wales Path. (Here you have the option of extending the walk to the Druids Circle, by continuing ahead on the track, past a waymarker post at point **2** of **Walk 19**, and following a path up the small ridge.) For the main walk follow the green track (and waymarked North Wales Path) west – *enjoying extensive views across the wild upland landscape grazed by ponies. Looking towards the Northern Carneddau the line of pylons mark the route of a Roman*

Follow the road down to a junction. Turn LEFT and continue along the quiet country road to eventually reach the entrance to Nant y Coed Nature Reserve on a sharp bend. Follow the North Wales Path across a footbridge over the Afon Llanfairfechan to another road. Follow it RIGHT, soon passing a side road. Continue along the road after the North Wales Path leaves it to eventually reach Bron Cae cottages – *with a good view overlooking Llanfairfechan.*

5 At the far end go down a single track road on the right. Keep ahead at a junction to the road's end by houses, then continue along an enclosed path, soon descending a handrailed section. Go past a path on the left and one angling back on the right. Just beyond turn LEFT along a narrow lane between houses. Cross a road and go down the lane opposite, past a side road, then take a short path ahead beyond garages to emerge on Llannerch road opposite Woden House. Follow it RIGHT bending up past a side road and a churchyard. Shortly, take a signposted path on the left by Gwesty Pen-y-Bryn. Follow the enclosed path behind the pub and past the church, and on down to cross a footbridge over the river, to almost unexpectedly arrive back at your starting point.

FOEL LWYD & MOELFRE

DESCRIPTION A 7½ mile walk for experienced walkers exploring wild upland pasture, moorland and mountain terrain. After passing through Nant y Coed Nature Reserve, the route heads towards Bwlch y Ddeufaen, then climbs Foel Lwyd (1978 feet/603 metre). After descending to the bwlch below Tal-y-fan, it heads northwards on a steady descent, later on an unmarked green track, then a path to a point overlooking the Druids Circle. After visiting the nearby small top of Moelfre (1427 feet/435 metres) and an aircraft crash memorial, the route returns with the North Wales Path on a long steady descent by track and road. Allow about 5 hours. Avoid in poor visibility.

START Nant y Coed, Llanfairfechan [SH 695740] or [SH 698736]

DIRECTIONS Turn off the A55 into Llanfairfechan. At traffic lights turn up Village Road, past shops and the school, then turn left up Bryn Road, soon becoming Valley Road. After the last houses continue ahead up Newry Drive to reach a small parking area on the sharp bend by Nant y Coed Information board. An alternative car park lies at the end of a no through road, accessed from a side road from Newry Drive.

I Enter Nant y Coed and go along the path, soon alongside the Afon Llanfairfechan. Shortly follow the waymarked path away from the river to pass the small fish pond, then cross the river by large stepping stones to a kissing gate. Turn LEFT and follow the path near the river, through a kissing gate, over a side stream and up to a car park. At its entrance, turn LEFT along a track adjoining the gated entrance to Camarnaints. After a kissing gate follow the track to cross the river. (The next section is guided by stone posts.) Go up the track's RIGHT fork then turn LEFT up the signed path along the edge of a side valley beneath the scree-covered slopes of Dinas. *On its top is an Iron Age hillfort containing the remains of hut circles.* Cross a green track and continue up the path, soon bending left

with the boundary up to an old stile/low boulder wall. The path continues up by a reedy stream to a kissing gate/gate into open country.

2 Continue ahead to pass a stone post to join a green track which rises steadily up across the reedy/stone covered upland pasture. Shortly it levels out and crosses a stream, then rises again to a kissing gate/gate. Follow a path up to post no. 3, then continue with a rough green track past an area of reeds, then ahead across the gorse covered upland pasture by Cwm Ddu towards a group of distant pylons at Bwlch y Ddeufaen. After another post the track passes through a wet reedy area then becomes a path which continues through gorse and passes a cross-path. Shortly when the path fades you have a choice: either keep ahead through gorse then reedy terrain, or follow a path LEFT through gorse to join a quad track which skirts the base of Foel Lwyd's western slopes.

3 Just before the large pylon head up the hillside round an area of gorse to join the wall rising up Foel Lwyd. Follow a path near the wall as it meanders up the stone covered slopes to the unmarked summit – *offering extensive views.* Continue on a path following the wall down Foel Lwyd's heather-covered eastern slopes – *with the rocky ridge of Tal-y-fan ahead* – to reach a ladder-stile at the bwlch. Turn LEFT and follow a path along the edge of a reedy area, then on a steady descent through heather. Later the path angles LEFT across a wet reedy area and a stream to join a good path at the end of a rocky knoll. Descend the meandering path, then after about 100 yards it bends half-RIGHT towards a small heather ridge. Keep

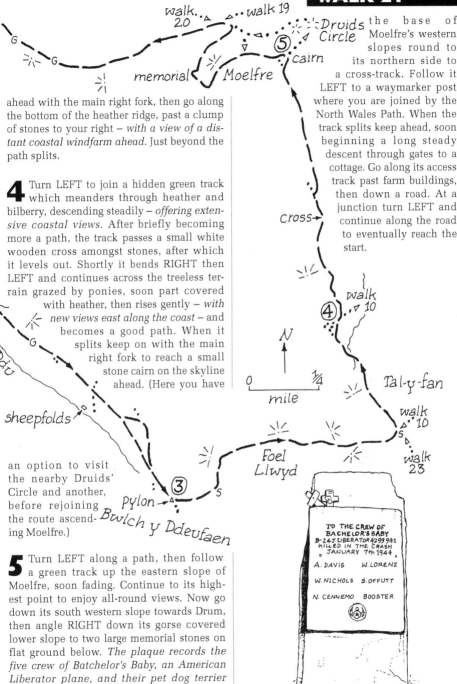

the base of Moelfre's western slopes round to its northern side to a cross-track. Follow it LEFT to a waymarker post where you are joined by the North Wales Path. When the track splits keep ahead, soon beginning a long steady descent through gates to a cottage. Go along its access track past farm buildings, then down a road. At a junction turn LEFT and continue along the road to eventually reach the start.

ahead with the main right fork, then go along the bottom of the heather ridge, past a clump of stones to your right – *with a view of a distant coastal windfarm ahead.* Just beyond the path splits.

4 Turn LEFT to join a hidden green track which meanders through heather and bilberry, descending steadily – *offering extensive coastal views.* After briefly becoming more a path, the track passes a small white wooden cross amongst stones, after which it levels out. Shortly it bends RIGHT then LEFT and continues across the treeless terrain grazed by ponies, soon part covered with heather, then rises gently – *with new views east along the coast* – and becomes a good path. When it splits keep on with the main right fork to reach a small stone cairn on the skyline ahead. (Here you have

an option to visit the nearby Druids' Circle and another, before rejoining the route ascending Moelfre.)

5 Turn LEFT along a path, then follow a green track up the eastern slope of Moelfre, soon fading. Continue to its highest point to enjoy all-round views. Now go down its south western slope towards Drum, then angle RIGHT down its gorse covered lower slope to two large memorial stones on flat ground below. *The plaque records the five crew of Batchelor's Baby, an American Liberator plane, and their pet dog terrier 'Booster', killed in a crash on Jan 7th 1944.* Return a few yards then follow a path along

TO THE CREW OF
BACHELOR'S BABY
B-24J LIBERATOR 4299 991
KILLED IN THE CRASH
JANUARY 7th 1944

A. DAVIS   W. LORENZ

W. NICHOLS   S. OFFUTT

N. CENNEMO   BOOSTER

NANT Y COED

DESCRIPTION A 2 mile walk exploring the delightful wooded valley of Nant y Coed Nature Reserve – popular with visitors since the late 19thC – and adjoining countryside. Allow about 2 hours.

START Nant y Coed, Llanfairfechan [SH 695740]

DIRECTIONS See **Walk 21**.

1 Go through the kissing gate into Nant y Coed and follow the stony path, soon alongside the Afon Llanfairfechan. Shortly follow the waymarked path away from the river to pass the small fish pond. When you rejoin the river, take the waymarked circular route on the left (optional). The zig-zag path climbs through the trees. At a path junction keep ahead and follow the delightful path up across the attractive oak and scree covered steep slopes, before descending on the panoramic return route. After rejoining the river cross it by large stepping stones to a kissing gate. Turn LEFT and follow the path near the river and on to a kissing gate. Cross a side stream by stepping stones and go up to a car park. At its entrance turn RIGHT along the narrow road.

2 Shortly take a signposted path on the left up to gates and continue along the green track. Go up a driveway past a house, then along a narrow path ahead past an outbuilding to a kissing gate. Follow the path up across the steep slope and through a gateway ahead. Go along the right-hand field edge, through a gap in the corner and on along the top edge of the next field to a kissing gate. Go down the access track to a road. Follow it RIGHT. At a junction keep ahead up the No Through road, then on the bend take the North Wales Path on the left to cross a footbridge by the start.

BWLCH Y DDEUFAEN & FOEL LWYD

DESCRIPTION An 8 mile walk **(A)** for experienced walkers exploring the foothills of the northern Carneddau. The route rises across Garreg Fawr to join an ancient upland road, once a Roman Road (See **Walk 27**), which it follows east to Bwlch y Ddeufaen and passes two standing stones. Later it climbs Foel Lwyd (1978 feet/603 metres), descends its western slope then heads along Cwm Ddu, later descending to Nant y Coed and continuing across country. Avoid in poor visibility. Allow about 5 hours. The route also includes a less demanding 6 mile **(B)** walk omitting Foel Lwyd.

START Valley Road, Llanfairfechan [SH 688742]

DIRECTIONS See **Walk 26**.

1 Follow instructions in paragraph **1** of **Walk 26**.

2 Turn LEFT up the track to the large pylon then go up the track's left fork to a finger post at a crossroad of tracks. Turn LEFT signposted to Rowen and follow the upland stony track, the former Roman Road, eastwards for 1¼ mile to a ladder-stile/ gate at Bwlch y Ddeufaen *(the pass of two stones – allegedly dropped by a female giant on route to Ireland)*. Follow the track down past one standing stone to the more impressive lower one. (For **Walk B**, just beyond do a sharp U-turn left up a green track, then follow a path to a hidden ladder-stile. Continue to the large pylon ahead to join Walk A at point **3**.) For **Walk A** continue with the track beneath the rocky slopes of Foel Lwyd to reach a small car park, then go along the minor road past a stone circle – *with increasingly good views along the Conwy Valley.* After just over ½ mile take a signposted path over a ladder-stile on the left. Follow the path up the hillside, over ladder-stiles, to the bwlch between Tal-y-fan and Foel Lwyd. Turn LEFT and follow a path near the wall up the heather covered slopes of Foel Lwyd to its unmarked summit – *offering extensive coastal and mountain views.* Follow the wall down the western slopes, later passing a ladder-stile and continuing down towards pylons below. After passing an old spoil heap angle away from the wall down round gorse to the large pylon below. Turn RIGHT.

3 Head towards the distant quarried hill on the skyline ahead, soon joining a quad track, which passes through a wet reedy area then continues beneath the western slopes of Foel Lwyd. After passing through another reedy area take the first of two paths on the left across the reedy, then gorse terrain. When you are looking down into the side valley of Cwm Ddu, follow a path leading RIGHT through gorse. Go over a cross-path and continue with a green track, passing through a wet reedy area, to reach a stone post. Either continue ahead along the reedy track or turn LEFT as signposted to join a nearby cross-path. Follow it RIGHT parallel with the nearby track to another stone post no. 3, then follow the track down to a kissing gate/gate. Continue down the green track, soon levelling out and crossing a stream.

4 After another post, as the faint track angles down towards a gate, keep ahead past a further stone post to a kissing gate/ gate. *(The next section is guided by further stone posts. Ahead is the scree-covered Dinas, on whose top is an Iron Age hillfort containing the remains of hut circles.)* Continue down beside a reedy stream to an old stile, then follow the wall down the edge of the reedy field. In the corner, turn RIGHT down a sunken path, then at a green track go through the gap ahead and follow the signed path LEFT above an attractive wooded side valley, soon descending to join a stony track. Follow it down to cross a bridge over a river, then follow the green track to a kissing gate to join a minor road by a car park at Nant y Coed. Follow it along the valley. Now follow instructions in paragraph **2** of **Walk 22** across country down to a road, then follow it west to join your outward stepped path.

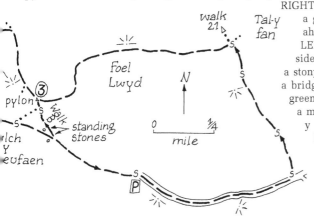

walk 21

Tal-y fan

Foel Lwyd

N

pylon ③

standing stones

Bwlch Y Ddeufaen

0   ¼   mile

WALK 24

FOEL GANOL

DESCRIPTION A 7 mile upland walk for experienced hill walkers featuring one of the best small ridges in Snowdonia, offering stunning views. The route follows the North Wales Path up to the former Roman Road, then a green track up to Foel Dduarth. After climbing nearby Foel Ganol (1765 feet/536 metres) you follow an undulating route across two further small tops then return down a stony track (offering an optional extension up to Drum) and an alternative route across Garreg Fawr. Allow about 5 hours. Avoid in poor visibility.

START Valley Road. Llanfairfechan [SH 688742]

DIRECTIONS See **Walk 26**.

1 Follow the side road over the river, then turn LEFT between garages and go up a stepped path to a road above. Follow it LEFT then take the signposted North Wales Path on the right to a ladder-stile in the right hand field corner. Follow the enclosed path up to another ladder-stile. The NWP now angles up the hillside to a kissing gate and continues up past stone post no. 9 and a nearby old settlement site, then past side paths. The NWP, now a more distinctive green track, briefly joins a wall, then rises across Garreg Fawr and continues to a large pylon. Here, take the track's right fork, past a smaller pylon, to reach the Roman road. Descend the stony track, soon levelling out.

2 Before the track bends down right go up a green track on the left. It soon levels out, then rises in stages across the northern slopes of Foel Ganol grazed by ponies. As it bends left up towards the nearby ridge continue ahead up the slope to reach the craggy top of Foel Dduarth, offering dramatic views down into Cwm Anafon. Return along the ridge then climb up the western slope of Foel Ganol to its heather top. A path now descends to a broad heather covered area containing a tiny pool, then bears LEFT up a ridge onto Yr Orsedd and continues along its narrow grassy ridge. Just before its end the

path descends LEFT, soon levelling out.

3 The path then rises again onto Pen Bryn-Ddu to reach a small stone cairn -with a good view of Llyn Anafon reservoir and the track rising towards Drum. Follow the path down and on past side paths to join the nearby stony track. Follow it back across the hillside, later descending steadily to reach a signposted crossroad of tracks. Follow the track ahead signposted to Llanfairfechan down to join your outward route at the pylon. Descend to a crossroad of tracks. Here angle RIGHT to follow a delightful green track across the eastern slopes of Garreg Fawr, later bending down across its northern slopes, soon alongside a wall. Just after the wall bends right, the green track continues ahead down through gorse to rejoin the NWP. Turn RIGHT.

4 Follow the NWP down to the kissing gate. After descending past the seat, turn sharp LEFT down the wide side path to a fence corner. Here turn sharp LEFT down to pass behind Tanrallt Ucha to a kissing gate. Follow the enclosed path to the nearby driveway which you follow down to the road. Follow it RIGHT to join your outward stepped path.

WALK 25

FOEL GANOL & CWM ANAFON

DESCRIPTION A 7¾ mile (**A**) or 8 mile (**B**) walk for experienced hill walkers featuring one of Snowdonia best small ridges and a stunning upland valley. The route follows Walk 24 up to Foel Ganol, then just below Yr Orsedd, it descends into Cwm Anafon. **Walk A** follows the track around Foel Dduarth, then a path across upland pasture. **Walk B** follows the river, then the North Wales Path. Both then follow a different route back across the edge of Garreg Fawr. Allow about 5½ hours.

START As **Walk 24**.

30

WALKS 24 & 25

1-2 Follow instructions in paragraphs **1-2** of **Walk 24**.

3 At a clear cross path follow it RIGHT down the top of the tussocky side valley, past a small stone sheepfold and a large boulder below. Continue down just to the right of a reedy area, then cross a small reedy gully. Here turn RIGHT and follow the reeds across the hillside to unexpectedly join a wide green path. It descends past old workings then levels out and disappears in reeds. Just beyond descend to the bottom of another reedy area at the head of a small side valley, then descend it towards stone sheepfolds in Cwm Anafon below. Follow the track through the valley beneath Foel Ganol. After the track briefly descends you have a choice. (For **Walk B** take a path on the left to closely follow the river. Later near a forest corner follow a wall away from the river to reach a descending stony track. Go up the track (NWP), soon bending left and continuing up near a wall. It then heads east and rises steadily to join **Walk A** at point **5**.)

to pass beneath stone enclosures. Walk along the right hand side of a small reedy gully then bend round a reedy area from where a path continues across the lower northern slopes of Foel Ganol, later rising to join the Roman road and **Walk B**.

5 Go up the track, soon joining your outward route. About 20 yards further angle LEFT to follow a path through gorse then beneath pylons, becoming a green track. At a track junction near your outward route turn LEFT and follow the track down the hillside towards

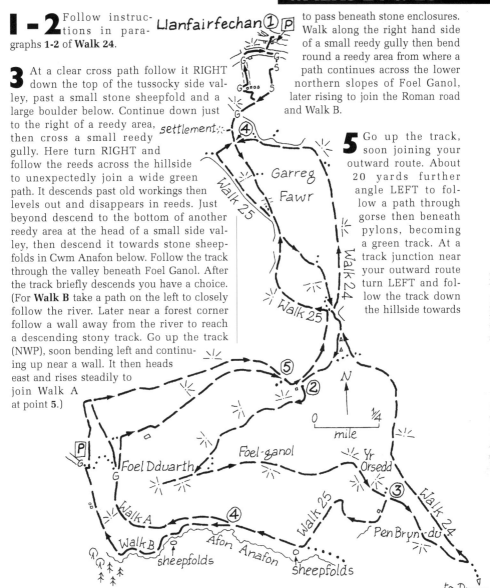

4 For **Walk A** continue along the track, which rises steadily beneath Foel Dduarth then levels out and reaches an old gateway. (An option here is to continue along the track past a descending track to join Walk B.) Take a path on the right angling across the gorse covered hillside, soon bending RIGHT up another sunken green path and on

Anglesey. It then levels out and continues briefly near a wall before rising to join your outward route at a wall corner. Keep alongside the wall, soon following another green track down the hillside. When both bend left turn RIGHT up a path through gorse to rejoin the NWP. Now follow instructions in paragraph **4** of **Walk 24**.

31

WALK 26

GARREG FAWR

DESCRIPTION A 3¼ mile **(A)** or 3 mile **(B)** walk using the network of delightful green paths and tracks to explore the small hill of Garreg Fawr (1194 feet/ 364 metres), now an Open Access area, offering panoramic views. Walk A visits its craggy top, then returns with Walk B down the North Wales Path. Allow about 2–2½ hours.

START Valley Road, Llanfairfechan [SH 688742]

DIRECTIONS Turn off the A55 into Llanfairfechan. At traffic lights turn up Village Road, passing the school and shops. At a junction, turn left up Bryn Road, soon becoming Valley Road to find a large parking area on the right by a side road at the last houses.

I Follow the side road across a bridge over the river, then turn LEFT between garages and go up a stepped path to a road above. Follow it west past Bron Cae cottages then take a signposted path up the driveway to Tanrallt Ucha. On the bend follow a waymarked enclosed path to a kissing gate, then behind the farm. Just before a fence corner turn RIGHT and follow a wide green path up the gorse/bracken covered hillside to a path junction. Turn RIGHT and follow another delightful path up to a kissing gate. Turn LEFT and follow the wall up the gorse covered hillside towards the craggy top of Garreg Fawr. At the top wall corner continue along a level narrow green track above the wall, soon rising steadily then heading south and levelling out – *offering a panorama of mountains*. Continue with the green track's right fork across the eastern slopes of Garreg Fawr to eventually reach a junction of tracks at a NWP waymarker post.

2 Turn sharp RIGHT and follow the North Wales Path north. At the next waymarker post the track splits. (For **Walk B** continue with the NWP down its left fork.) For **Walk A** take the right fork and follow the meandering green track across the wide flattish top of Garreg Fawr to reach its craggy

top. Keep ahead down the slope towards Llanfairfechan, passing a fence protecting a sharp drop, then descend to a wide green cross-path. Follow it LEFT. After about 45 yards turn LEFT past stone post no. 8 and continue below stone sheepfolds and Garreg Fawr's western slopes. At another stone post, descend to a nearby wooden waymarker post to rejoin the North Wales Path. Follow it down through gorse, past side paths, stone post no. 9 and a nearby old settlement site, to the kissing gate. Go down your outward route past the seat, then keep ahead down to a ladder-stile. Follow the enclosed path down to another ladder-stile, then go across a field to a road. Follow it LEFT back to your outward stepped path.

WALK 27

ROMAN ROAD

DESCRIPTION A 6 mile walk featuring attractive upland pasture, delightful green tracks on Garreg Fawr, a section of a former Roman Road, which it joins at a height of 1279 feet, and extensive views. Allow about 4 hours. The walk can be accessed from Bont Newydd, Abergwyngregyn or a small road end car park as shown.

START Valley Road, Llanfairfechan [SH 688742]

DIRECTIONS See **Walk 26**.

B*eneath the foot-* Abergwyngreg *hills of the northern Carneddau is a prehistoric mountain trackway which* Bont *became part of a Roman road* Newydd *which ran from Canovium fort in the Conwy Valley to Segontium in Caernarfon. Later it became an important drovers route, with Aber serving as a stopping station. Traditionally, these upland pastures were grazed by cattle during the summer, but by the early 19thC, sheep had taken over. Wild ponies still graze here.*

I Follow the side road across a bridge over the river, then turn LEFT between garages and go up a stepped path to a road above. Follow the road (Terrace Walk) west past Bron Cae cottages. After ⅓ mile the road bends left. At a house, go through a bridle-gate and follow the enclosed rock based track up to a kissing gate/gate. Continue with the green track, soon rising away from the wall up the gorse covered hillside. It then follows another wall up into open country, later joining the waymarked North Wales Path. This delightful narrow green track rises across the slopes of Garreg Fawr, then continues to a junction of tracks at a waymarker post near a wall corner.

3 Before power cables, cross a stone stile on the left. Follow the path up the bracken covered slope ahead to a level path just to the left of the large pylon base. Here angle LEFT up to join a higher cross path leading from the top pylon foot. Follow it across the steep gorse covered hillside – *soon with a view to Anglesey*. The path rises gently to cross exposed rocks then contours across less steep terrain and passes through bracken towards the large wall ahead. Take its less distinct right fork to pass just to the right of a solitary tree ahead. Now angle RIGHT up a path, soon joining another. Just before the wall turn RIGHT up to a ladder-stile. Continue ahead beside the wall down two fields.

4 After crossing an iron ladder-stile go slightly RIGHT down the large field to join the distant wall ahead. Follow it down to cross a ladder-stile in the corner onto a green track below. Follow a path opposite down through trees to stepping stones over the river, then up to a kissing gate. Go half-LEFT across the field to a ladder-stile/gate, then go down the lane. On the bend take a signposted path on the right to a kissing gate. Follow the fence down and round beneath the bracken/gorse-covered hillside to a gate by a house. Go along a green track, through another gate then follow Llys-y-Gwynt farm's access track ahead to join a road. Shortly, turn RIGHT up Terrace Walk, soon joining your outward route.

2 Follow the stony track ahead up to a large pylon. Take the track's right fork up past another pylon to a stony track – *the Roman Road*. Turn RIGHT and follow the track on a steady descent in stages westwards towards Aber. After 1 mile the track bends south beside a large wall, soon descending then bending down to a gate. Go along the narrow walled road, soon descending.

COEDYDD ABER

DESCRIPTION A 5¾ mile (**A**) walk through the Coedydd Aber National Nature Reserve, featuring the stunning Aber Falls (Rhaedr Fawr) in its magnificent mountain setting. The route takes the popular trail to Aber Falls, then passes another waterfall, before making a steady ascent across open slopes. It then follows a highly scenic upland section of the North Wales Path, offering extensive coastal views, before descending a side valley and following field paths to Abergwyngregyn. Allow about 3½ hours. The route includes a shorter 3¾ mile (**B**) walk and a simple 2½ mile circuit (**C**) to Aber Falls.

START Bont Newydd, Abergwyngregyn [SH 662720]

DIRECTIONS Turn off the A55 signposted to Abergwyngregyn, and follow the road south through the village and along the wooded valley to reach a parking area just before the road crosses the river (Bont Newydd). An alternative Aber Forestry Commission car park/toilets is signposted from the other side of the bridge. Both car parks are pay and display. (From the forestry car park return down the road, then take the signposted path to Aber Falls to cross a footbridge over the river, and up through the trees. Go along the forestry track ahead to gates. Follow the green track down to join the stony track by an information board.) An alternative start can be made from the free village car park (See Walk 29).

Coedydd Aber, managed by the Countryside Council for Wales, is located in a steep-sided valley between the Carneddau mountains and the coastal plain. Extensive archaeological remains, including prehistoric burial and settlement sites, reveal man's association with this sheltered valley and surrounding uplands for over 3000 years. Its dense mixed woodland is now the home of both woodland and mountain birds. The famous waterfall, formed during the Ice Age, has attracted visitors since the late 18thC, aided by the opening of the post road in the 1820s and the railway in 1848. The river rises as Yr Afon Goch (red river) and flows over the 100 foot rock face to become Afon Rhaedr Fawr (the river of the great falls) which flows down to the sea. It is one of the steepest rivers from source to mouth in England and Wales.

I Go through the kissing gate at the end of Bont Newydd (the new bridge) built in the 1820s to enter Coedydd Aber. Follow the path alongside the river. After crossing a footbridge over the river, go through a small gate, then turn RIGHT up a stony track. Keep with the main track signposted to the waterfall, as it climbs steadily up the increasingly open wooded valley, soon giving views to the mountains ahead, to reach Nant Rhaedr Visitor Centre. *This was originally a Welsh tyddyn (smallholding), which once sold tea and home-made lemonade to Victorian visitors on route to the Falls, and now contains an exhibition.* Continue along the wide stony path and suddenly, the impressive waterfall comes into view. The path now narrows and continues up to a small gate and on to reach the base of the waterfall. (Retrace your steps then for **Walk C**, return to the gate, cross the nearby ladder-stile, and follow the way-marked path angling up the rocky slope to a ladder-stile into the forest. Follow the path through the forest, then alongside its boundary to rejoin your outward route.)

2 For **Walk A**, cross the footbridge over the river. Follow the path up above the river to a close viewpoint of the waterfall, then go to a nearby gate and follow the waymarked North Wales Path, soon alongside a wall beneath impressive crags. After passing a ladder-stile the path descends to a footbridge over a river beneath another waterfall. The path now continues over several streams, later bending north and rising steadily up the part bracken covered slope and on across the hillside to reach a ladder-stile/gate. Continue up a green track, past a seat – *a good stopping place* – to another ladder-stile. The track continues up to a further ladder-stile, then passes beneath power cables. Shortly the track makes a gentle descent – *with new views to Anglesey, Puffin Island and east along the coast to the*

34

Abergwyngregyn

Bont Newydd

N

walk 29

pylon

Afon Rhaeadr-Fawr

② Rhaeadr Fawr
Falls   Aber Falls

④ walk 29

Great Orme – and passes a seat to go through a nearby gate beneath a plantation. Continue along the green track to gates at a prominent viewpoint.

3 Here the track splits. (For **Walk B**, take the stony track down the hillside. At a waymarker post turn right, and follow a path angling down the steep slope to reach the road.) Follow the level green track on the waymarked NWP through gates ahead, then across the hillside to a kissing gate. Continue ahead alongside the fence – *enjoying panoramic coastal views* – to a ladder-stile. Keep ahead. After another ladder-stile follow the faint green track passing above a steep side valley. Just before the next ladder-stile bend RIGHT with the track.

4 Follow the improving track down the hillside towards the coast into the side valley, over a stream and through a gate into a field. Leave the track and go down the left field edge to a ladder-stile near a cottage. Go down its access track, then after about 30 yards, at a waymarker post in the roots of a large tree, turn RIGHT up the bank. Go across the field, over a ladder-stile ahead, and on across the next field to another ladder-stile. Continue by trees above farm buildings, then angle down through the trees to a gate at the end of outbuildings. Go ahead between the house and an outbuilding through gates into a field. Go ahead across the field to a ladder-stile/gate by attractive slate fencing. Continue ahead along a faint track to a kissing gate/gate by a descending track. Go down the green track to a kissing gate by a cottage, and on over a ladder-stile ahead. Go across the field to a kissing gate, then along the next field edge to another kissing gate.

5 Follow the path across the bracken-covered slope overlooking Abergwyngregyn, past a seat, after which it gently descends. When it splits continue on the upper right fork between fences to a gate and on down to the road. Follow it back to the start.

WALK 29

GYRN & MOEL WNION

DESCRIPTION A 7¾ mile **(A)** or 6¾ mile **(B)** walk for experienced hill walkers exploring the wild upland landscape beyond Abergwyngregyn, featuring two outlying hills at the edge of Snowdonia National Park and panoramic views throughout. After an early steep climb the route rises across upland pasture to follow a delightful path across the eastern slopes of Moel Wnion. It continues across an upland plateau to visit Gyrn (1778 feet/542 metres) then climbs nearby Moel Wnion (1902 feet/580 metres). **Walk A** returns to follow old tracks down and across the lower slopes of Moel Wnion to join the North Wales Path. **Walk B** makes a more demanding descent from Moel Wnion (good navigation required) to rejoin the main route. The walk either continues along the panoramic upland North Wales Path (**route A**) to descend your outward route, or descends earlier to follow a lower level section (**route B**). Allow about 5 hours. Avoid in poor visibility. **START** Abergwyngregyn [SH 656728]
DIRECTIONS Turn off the A55 to Abergwyngregyn. Turn left past the bus stop, over the river to find a formal roadside car park.

A *bergwyngregyn (the estuary of the white shells), originally known as Aber Garth was once an important settlement. It stands at the end of an ancient mountain highway, later a Roman Road from the Conwy Valley which extended across the sands to Beaumaris. In the 13thC it was a favourite manor of the Princes of Gwynedd. According to legend, it was here that Llywelyn the Great imprisoned his wife Joan, the daughter of England's King John, and hanged William de Breos, Prince of Powys after discovering their affair. In the 18thC it was an important stopping place for drovers, with many inns.*

I Return along the road and after crossing the river then take a signposted path on the left past toilets/information centre to a

road. Follow it ahead and at the junction turn left. Follow the road past Yr Hen Felin Cafe & Information Centre, then take a signposted path through a small gate up on the right. Go up its left fork which rises steeply up the hillside to a small gate, then continues up to a waymarked path junction at a stony track. Follow it up the hillside to join the North Wales Path at the top.

2 Go through a small gate head and follow the delightful green track towards a panorama of mountains to gates below a plantation. From the plantation corner angle up the hillside to pass above a large pylon and on to a ladder-stile ahead – *enjoying good views to Aber Falls and surrounding mountains.* Head in the same direction up the hillside, shortly levelling out and continuing beneath an incoming wall to cross a ladder-stile by a small gate and sheepfolds into Open Access land. Go up past the side of the sheepfolds to a crosspath above. Follow it LEFT above the sheepfolds then continue ahead along a delightful green path across the mid slopes of Moel Wnion – *offering panoramic views of mountains and hidden valleys.* Later it descends to cross a stream by a hawthorn tree.

3 About 30 yards beyond the path splits. Ignore the one descending into the valley, but take its higher right fork passing beneath the nearby small scree slope. Follow it across the hillside, over two streams beneath old workings, and on through bracken onto a ridge overlooking the side valley. Follow its right fork up the ridge and across a reedy area. After a tiny scree slope when the path fades, keep ahead up through another reedy area onto the high ground ahead. Now angle RIGHT up the hillside. Shortly the terrain levels out providing views of distant mountains, and the nearby small stone covered hill of Gyrn, with its complex of stone sheepfolds. Continue across the tussocky ground towards Gyrn, over an old cross track and on to pass to the right of the fence/ sheepfolds up to a small stone shelter on its top – *offering extensive views from Snowdon to Holyhead Mountain.* Return down the slope and just to the left of the sheepfolds follow

36

a clear path straight ahead, keeping with its right fork to join the stony cross track.

4 To visit Moel Wnion keep ahead to follow a quad track up onto its broad flat top to a stone shelter on the site of a larger ancient circular cairn. (For **Walk B** angle left across the short tussocky terrain and descend its north western slopes, later following a stream to a wall corner below. Follow the wall left to join the main walk at the iron ladder-stile.) For **Walk A** return down to the stony track, then follow it on a long steady descent towards the end of the Menai Straits – *with Penrhyn Castle and Bangor pier prominent*. Later the track descends past a reedy gully and side paths. When level with a boundary wall corner about 150 yards to your left you pass through a short sunken section of track. At its end turn RIGHT to follow an old green track across the part gorse covered lower slopes of Moel Wnion, later becoming a path, to cross an old iron ladder-stile in the wall corner. Cross the stream below, then go up the slope to pass a small tree. Angle LEFT down the field to join a track and the North Wales Path. Follow it to gates by pylons, then go down the field edge to a ladder-stile.

5 Here you have a choice.

Route A: Keep ahead to follow the intermittent green track across upland pasture, crossing two ladder-stiles, passing through a kissing gate, then a gate to join your outward route at point **2**.

Route B: Turn LEFT on a green track, then follow instructions in paragraph **4** of Walk 28. After the kissing gate follow the path across the bracken-covered slope overlooking Abergwyngregyn and past a seat, then go down its left fork to a ladder-stile. Follow the nearby house's access track to the road in the village.

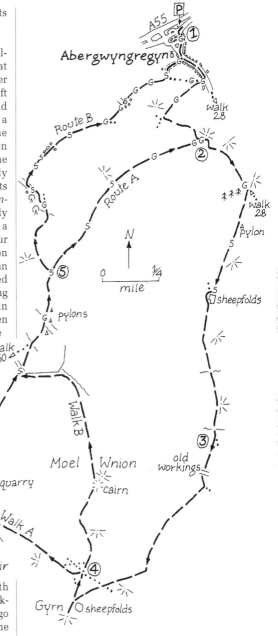

Traeth Lafan (Lavan Sands) lying between Llanfairfechan and Bangor, is a designated Special Site of Scientific Interest and a Special Protection Area. It attracts huge flocks of birds, including many species of wildfowl and wading birds during spring and autumn migration, and large numbers of overwintering waders. The sand, shingle, saltmarsh and extensive mudflats exposed at low tide stretching over towards Anglesey, offer an abundance of food – i.e. ragworms, snails, cockles, and mussels, as well as fish – that attract and sustain a wide variety of birds. The Spinnies and Morfa Aber Nature Reserves contain hides for the discreet viewing of birds.

T R A E T H   L A F A N

Aber Ogwen
P ①
N
0 ¼ mile
The Spinnies
Crymr Farm
A55
④ Tan-y-Lon
Hendre
Coed Ty'n -yr hendre
Bronydd Isaf

I Head east from the car park to follow the coastal path along the shingle shoreline – *with views across to Beaumaris and Puffin island.* As you pass round beneath small cliffs, new views unfold along the coast to the Great Orme. The path then continues on grass past a small wood, and on alongside an attractive slate boundary. Follow the grassy foreshore to its end, then continue along the rocky shore. *In 1648, this area was the scene of a battle, known as Y Dalar Hir (the long front) which saw Parliamentarian troops defeat Royalist forces.* After crossing a stream, go up onto a grass embankment to soon join an access track by a house. *Prior to the building of Telford's suspension bridge over the Menai Straits in 1826, crossing to and from the mainland was hazardous. Mail and travellers to Anglesey and Ireland were ferried from near here to Beaumaris. Cattle would be driven across Traeth Lafan when the channel was at its narrowest, risking quicksand and the ravages of the fast incoming tide.* Follow the track to Morfa Aber reserve.

2 Go along the road, passing under the railway. At a junction, continue up the road. At the next junction, turn LEFT towards Abergwyngregyn to pass under the A55. Turn LEFT. (For the low level road alternative turn right.) Shortly turn RIGHT, signposted to Aber Falls, then take the next road on the right through the village, past Yr Hen Felin Café & Information Centre, then just past Nant y Felin on the left take a signposted path through a small gate up on the right. Go up its left fork which rises steeply up the hillside to a small gate. *Here are extensive views over Traeth Lafan and along the coast from the Great Orme to Bangor.* Continue up the path to a waymarked path junction at a stony track, then follow it up the hillside.

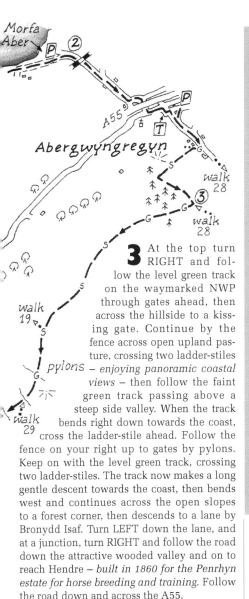

TRAETH LAFAN

DESCRIPTION A 7½ mile walk featuring a section of unspoilt coast, nature reserves, extensive birdlife, and foothills offering great views. The route follows the coastal path east for 3 miles along the shoreline of Traeth Lafan to Morfa Aber nature reserve, before heading inland to Abergwyngregyn. After a short steep climb to about 800 feet it then follows the scenic high-level North Wales Path across the open slopes of the northern Carneddau foothills, before descending to Tan-y-Lon and following field paths to The Spinnies nature reserve. Allow about 4½ hours. A lower level alternative to the North Wales Path section is to follow quiet lanes from Aber. Binoculars are recommended. Where possible, time your walk to avoid high tide in order not to disturb birds roosting on the narrow upper shore, and keep dogs under strict control.

START Aber Ogwen car park [SH 616724] or Abergwyngregyn [SH 656728]

DIRECTIONS From Bangor, turn off the A5122 by Penrhyn Castle towards Tal-y-Bont, passing over the river. Ignore turnings into Tal-y-Bont, then take a road on the left, signposted 'Nature Reserve'. Go past the reserve to the shore car park. For the alternative start from Abergwyngregyn see **Walk 29** then follow instructions in paragraph 1 to reach point 3 of this walk.

3 At the top turn RIGHT and follow the level green track on the waymarked NWP through gates ahead, then across the hillside to a kissing gate. Continue by the fence across open upland pasture, crossing two ladder-stiles – *enjoying panoramic coastal views* – then follow the faint green track passing above a steep side valley. When the track bends right down towards the coast, cross the ladder-stile ahead. Follow the fence on your right up to gates by pylons. Keep on with the level green track, crossing two ladder-stiles. The track now makes a long gentle descent towards the coast, then bends west and continues across the open slopes to a forest corner, then descends to a lane by Bronydd Isaf. Turn LEFT down the lane, and at a junction, turn RIGHT and follow the road down the attractive wooded valley and on to reach Hendre – *built in 1860 for the Penrhyn estate for horse breeding and training*. Follow the road down and across the A55.

4 Just before a junction at Tan-y-Lon, take a signposted path over a stile on the right. Bear RIGHT and follow the concrete track round to its end. Continue ahead along a green track, through a wood, under a railway line and over a stile into a field. Go half-RIGHT to cross a ladder-stile, then turn LEFT to walk along the field edge. Go through a kissing gate at the end of a small wood, then go straight across the next field and through a gate in the boundary ahead. Follow the boundary on your right, continuing with a track – *with Penrhyn Castle, built between 1819-35 from wealth accrued from the slate industry, prominent on the skyline* – to pass farm buildings. Follow the waymarked path through a gate, passing to the left of the house to a road. Turn RIGHT to reach the entrance to The Spinnies nature reserve. Follow the path through the reserve to the hide to watch the birds on the lagoon, then go through shrubs to reach the Ogwen estuary. Follow the shoreline back to the start.

PRONUNCIATION

Welsh	English equivalent
c	always hard, as in cat
ch	as in the Scottish word loch
dd	as th in then
f	as f in of
ff	as ff in off
g	always hard as in got
ll	no real equivalent. It is like 'th' in then, but with an 'L' sound added to it, giving 'thlan' for the pronunciation of the Welsh 'Llan'.

KEY TO THE MAPS

- → Walk route and direction
- ── Metalled road
- ─── Unsurfaced road
- •••• Footpath/route adjoining walk route
- ∿→ River/stream
- ⚘ ⚘ Trees
- ▄▄ Railway
- **G** Gate
- **S** Stile
- **F.B.** Footbridge
- ⟍⟋ Viewpoint
- **P** Parking
- **T** Telephone

THE COUNTRYSIDE CODE

- Be safe – plan ahead and follow any signs
- Leave gates and property as you find them
- Protect plants and animals, and take your litter home
- Keep dogs under close control
- Consider other people

Open Access
Some routes cross areas of land where walkers have the legal right of access under The CRoW Act 2000 introduced in May 2005. Access can be subject to restrictions and closure for land management or safety reasons for up to 28 days a year. Please respect any notices. The Countryside Council for Wales website (www.ccw.gov.uk) provides updated information on any closures.

Path problems

Please contact the local Highways Department regarding any path problems encountered:
Conwy County Borough Council   01492 574000 *(most walks)*
Gwynedd Council   01766 771000 *(for walks near Abergwyngregyn)*

About the author, David Berry

David is an experienced walker with a love of the countryside and an interest in local history. He is the author of a series of walks guidebooks covering North Wales, where he has lived and worked for many years, as well as a freelance writer for Walking Wales magazine. He has worked as a Rights of Way surveyor across North Wales and served as a member of Denbighshire Local Access Forum.

Whether on a riverside ramble, mountain or long distance walk, he greatly appreciates the beauty, culture and history of the landscape and hopes that his comprehensive guidebooks will encourage people to explore on foot its diverse scenery and rich heritage.

Published by **Kittiwake-Books Limited**
3 Glantwymyn Village Workshops, Glantwymyn, Machynlleth, Montgomeryshire SY20 8LY

© Text & map research: David Berry 2010
© Maps & illustrations: Kittiwake 2010
Drawings by Morag Perrott
Cover photos: Main – Looking down on Conwy Castle from Conwy Mountain. *Inset* – Wild ponies on Tal-y-fan. David Berry.
Care has been taken to be accurate.
However neither the author nor the publisher can accept responsibility for any errors which may appear, or their consequences. If you are in any doubt about access, check before you proceed.
Printed by MWL, Pontypool.
ISBN: **978 1 902302 85 0**